Devnaa's
INDIA

Delicious Vegetarian Home Cooking & Street Food

ROOPA RAWAL

Devnaa's
INDIA

Delicious Vegetarian Home Cooking & Street Food

ROOPA RAWAL

First Published in 2013 by Devnaa LLP

Office 6a, Popin Business Centre

South Way

London, HA9 0HF

Photography: Jay Rawal

Copyeditor: Zoe Perrett

Cover & Interior Design: Ketan Raval at www.amoveo.tv

Devnaa ® is a registered trademark of Devnaa LLP

A catalogue record for this book is available from the British Library.

ISBN-10: 0957094752

ISBN-13: 9780957094758

www.devnaa.com

DEDICATION

To the hero in our lives, the man with more knowledge about
India than anyone we know, and the greatest 'secret' chef –
this one is for you, Dad.

CONTENTS

INTRODUCTION

"You'll need a little more oil in that pan if you want those to cook perfectly..."
"I'd put in a touch more water for the right amount of steam..."

The above are typical phrases I would hear whilst passing through the kitchen of our family home to make my way into the garden. The culinary tutor was my mother, an exceptional Indian cook with over 50 years' cooking experience. Her apprentice was my sister, and co-author of this book, Roopa.
And she was a star pupil. As an adult, Roopa makes magical things happen with flavours. I'll think of a few random ingredients, and she'll find a way to make an extraordinary meal from them... With a little help from Mum's spice box.

Our family home has always provided a hub for celebrating birthdays, anniversaries, or any other excuse to get everyone together for notable conversation and some great Indian food. There's something very welcoming and informal about our home, a place where you feel at ease walking into the kitchen, grabbing a plate of garlic-chilli mogo, and heading out into the conservatory to chill with a cold drink.
One of the most famous celebratory starters in our home is Mum's samosas. A samosa is just one of those appetisers that's loved by everyone – triangles of crisp, flaky pastry filled with a soft, spicy mix of vegetables are by far the most popular savoury items at any event. I remember discovering as a child how good Mum's samosa filling was, and asking her to make it especially so I could eat it with chapattis at dinner time. Twenty five years on, things haven't changed. Mum still makes the samosa filling for me on an almost weekly basis, together with some piping hot chapattis, because she knows how much I adore the unorthodox combination! For me, that has always been the real beauty of food - observing, tasting, and then choosing a dish that becomes a lifelong companion; something that has an emotional attachment and holds great memories.

We all have them, whether it's your favourite type of daal, dhokra, or dabeli, they remind you of a special event or a place from your past. From a chef's perspective, I believe food is like art; learning the basic techniques before putting his or her own personality and emotion into each dish. Roopa's preferred way of serving chilli paneer, traditionally eaten from a small plate or bowl, is the perfect example - my sister's version comes on baby lettuce leaves with mint chutney. Her take on the dish brings a cool freshness to the spicy snack, and makes for wonderful presentation, too.

When we published our first book, we didn't anticipate that people from all over the world would read the dessert recipes we spent a year putting together; we just wrote it because we wanted to share our creations and allow a wider audience to experience the wonderful flavours themselves. Another year on, we're ready to do it all over again- and this time it's all about soul food. We want to share the glorious Indian food we've eaten every day at home, along with some special treats usually only found at parties and sold from street food stalls.

Whatever topics we turn to in future publications, I know that this one will remain closest to my heart, because of the fond memories evoked by the recipes. Memories of paratha, lemon pickle and chai for breakfast before school; celebration favourites like kachoris and crispy bhajia; and, of course, the Saturday afternoon daal makhani with aloo paratha, swiftly followed by a nap on the sofa! I hope this book creates some equally fond memories for you, too.

Share and enjoy,

Jay

Jay Rawal

Growing up in a large Indian family, I have always eaten traditional Indian food on an almost daily basis. My family originates from Gujarat in Western India, where the regional cuisine is generally quite light and mostly vegetarian. Gujarati meals consist mainly of delicately-spiced dry curries made with locally-grown green or root vegetables; and light, clear, almost broth-like daals made from pulses and leafy greens, served with wholewheat chapattis and rice.

Although I was spoiled with this delicious, wholesome cuisine daily, I always looked forward to the food served at festivals or on special occasions at home. It was at these times that the ladies of the house – my Grandma (Ba), Mum, and Aunts – would pull out all the stops to create the special, decadent dishes that my siblings and I so adored.

One of my favourite dishes has always been something Mum likes to make when we have guests visiting. Her Handwo recipe is simply divine, with a soft, spongy, moist, almost cake-like texture and a crispy, slightly salted top. My brother Jay always goes straight for the crispiest pieces along with a hot cup of chai. You'll find my Handwo recipe on page 52.

Indian cuisine has evolved since I was a child. The rise of 'fast food' culture in the West has seen a parallel rise of 'street-food' culture all across India. Every day in Mumbai, hundreds of roadside stands serve thousands of freshly-made, hot, spicy, tangy dishes delighting the taste buds of locals and tourists alike. These flavourful dishes are so delicious that the recipes; developed on the roadside from traditional, regional methods; have been taken back into homes and transformed into beautiful, sophisticated dinner party treats. I am excited to share this collection of recipes, which includes some of my favourite, traditional childhood treats, and also some new favourites that I delight in serving to my loved ones on special occasions. I've included everything from chutneys to main courses – and, of course, a few lovely desserts.

I'm hoping my guide to easy Indian soul food helps you to delight just as many hungry friends and relatives as my Mother and Grandmother have done. Even if you're a complete novice to Indian cooking, these recipes should help you create a meal or snack that you will be proud to serve and call your own.

Share & enjoy,

Roopa

Roopa Rawal

INDIAN KITCHEN ESSENTIALS

MASALA DABBA OR SPICE TIN

This is a staple of every Indian kitchen and if your intention is to cook Indian food on a regular basis, then I cannot recommend enough that you keep one of these to hand. It is essentially one large tin containing lots of smaller tins or fitted out with internal compartments– a section for every key dry spice. What you store in your dabba will vary according to your personal taste and which spices you use the most; but my own dabba contains the following ingredients, all of which are used extensively throughout this recipe book:

RED CHILLI POWDER

Made from dried red chillies which have been ground to a powder, the heat of chilli powder varies with every batch – always proceed with caution at first. Once you have gauged the strength of the chilli powder, you can be as adventurous as you like. Use the measurements I have provided as guidelines, and adjust the heat to your taste by adding more or less as you please.

TURMERIC POWDER

This is quite a bitter spice, mainly known for its healing properties according to Ayurvedic medicine. It is extremely potent and you will only need to add a small amount to intensify the colour of curries (as well as stain your fingers – always handle with a spoon!)

CORIANDER & CUMIN POWDER

This is very much the Gujarati in me coming through. It would be more technically correct to use coriander powder and cumin powder separately, blending the quantities according to each individual curry, but I was brought up using this. My Grandma used it, my Mum still uses it, and I will continue the tradition! If you prefer to do so, you can use the powders separately and adjust the recipes accordingly – however, I will happily admit to using the mixed powder, ready-blended and raring to go.

CUMIN SEEDS

More commonly known as 'jeera' in Indian cooking, these little brown seeds are full of essential oils which release an earthy, warm flavour when heated. The whole spice gives a softer flavour to the powder, which can be a bit too strong and bitter. For some recipes I first dry-roast the seeds and then grind them, using this powder for a deep, smoky effect.

CAROM SEEDS

Also known as 'ajwain', these are often consumed as a digestive aid and are mostly used in dishes which contain high levels of protein – like pulses and spinach. They have a very distinct, pungent aroma which, when placed in the spice tin, helps distinguish them from jeera – be careful not to mix the two up when cooking in a rush.

MUSTARD SEEDS

For Indian cooking, you need the dark brown or black variety of these seeds as they impart a stronger, more intense flavour than the lighter and larger yellow ones. The whole spice produces a complex, slightly nuttier flavour than the powdered spice - which is quite potently hot.

CINNAMON BARK, GREEN CARDAMOM, AND CLOVES

These whole spices are generally roasted and ground to create blends of 'garam masala' – a complex spice mix which is extremely pungent and brings a bitter-sweet heat to dishes. In this case, I prefer to use the whole spices to create a more balanced, subtle effect which does not dominate the dish, but instead works in harmony with the other ingredients.

I will occasionally deviate from these 'holy grail' spices and throw in ones specific to certain dishes; but as long as you have these to hand you shouldn't need many more. Where more specific spices are used, I have tried to provide alternative, store-cupboard substitutes in case you don't happen to have them to hand.

Always remember that most Indian recipes are very forgiving, and you can generally use the spices you like in the quantities you prefer. If you do not have a certain flavouring to hand, or dislike a spice, feel free to replace as you wish, or even just omit it entirely.

GREEN CHILLIES, GARLIC, AND GINGER

These are the main fresh spices used throughout this recipe collection. Unless otherwise stated, the chillies are the thin, green variety that is normally about 5-8 cm long. Quantities of garlic and ginger can be difficult to gauge so I usually chop them up quite finely in a blender or grate on a Microplane and then measure the amounts in teaspoons. That said, all of these ingredients are added to taste, so feel free to fine-tune the quantities to your own preferences.

TOMATOES

The richness in many of the recipes presented in this book is achieved using tangy gravies made from chopped tomatoes. You can either use a good-quality tinned variety or make your own by blanching large tomatoes, peeling them, and then blending. Alternatively, just add fresh chopped tomatoes – although the colour of the gravy will not be as intense, and you may need to add a little extra sugar or lemon depending on how sweet or tart your tomatoes are, the taste will be every bit as delicious.

EQUIPMENT

I have tried to avoid using too many pieces of specialist equipment in creating these recipes, but I do recommend the following items - some of which you are likely to already have in your kitchen cupboard:

LARGE NON-STICK WOK OR 'KARAHI'
To help cook curries with ease, and for cooking the occasional deep-fried snack.

HEAVY BASED PANS WITH LIDS
These pans will help stop curries from sticking or burning. They can also be adapted to do the job of pressure cookers or steamers if you don't have these items.

ROLLING PIN AND NON-STICK FRYING PAN OR HEAVY IRON SKILLET
For rolling out and cooking flatbreads.

PRESSURE COOKER
These help cook daals and pulses quickly, and can also substitute as steamers.

STEAMER
For creating light, steamed snacks like Dhokra.

CHUTNEYS

An Indian dinner table just doesn't look complete without a selection of beautifully-hued, fragrant condiments presented alongside the meal. These sauces are created to perfectly compliment the flavours of Indian food, and can be used for dipping, drizzling, or even spreading on your favourite snack to accentuate the taste. Most of these recipes are really quick and easy to create and use just a few simple ingredients and a blender; some require a little cooking to achieve a deep, earthy flavour.

Chilli & Garlic Chutney

(Serves 6)

This chutney makes a great dipping sauce for most of the recipes featured in the 'Snacks & Farsaan' chapter. It also tastes great spread on naan as a 'pizza sauce'. Just top leftover naan bread with the chutney and your favourite toppings, and grill to jazz them up a treat.

INGREDIENTS

3 large ripe tomatoes
4 tsp minced garlic
2 green chillies
20 g fresh coriander
Salt to taste
1 tbsp sugar
1 tsp lemon juice

METHOD

• Quarter the tomatoes and place them in a food processor along with the garlic.
• Roughly chop the chillies and coriander and add these to the food processor.
• Add the salt, sugar, and lemon juice, and then blend in the processor until you have fairly smooth chutney. You may find that you need to add a little water along the way to reach the desired consistency; if so, just add 1 tablespoon at a time and blend well between additions until it looks right.
• Refrigerate until ready to serve alongside snacks such as Dhokra and Bhajia.

Coriander Chutney

(Serves 4)

This beautiful, vivid green chutney packs a punch of flavour that makes it a thoroughly suitable condiment served with almost any food. My favourites with this are Dhokra and Bhajia. I would actually knight it as the 'tomato sauce' of Indian cuisine, as diners drizzle it over anything from snacks to curries, and even rice if it takes their fancy. It is always advisable to mix up a batch if having a dinner party and, as it's so easy to make, there are no excuses not to! For a slightly different twist to the below recipe, add some raw green mango for a sharper, creamier chutney.

INGREDIENTS

75 g fresh coriander
2 green chillies
Salt to taste
½ tbsp sugar
1 tbsp lemon juice
A little cold water

METHOD

• Roughly chop the coriander and chillies before placing them in a food processor – don't be afraid to use the stalks of the coriander, they contain lots of flavour.
• Blend until finely chopped.
• Add the salt, sugar, and lemon juice and continue to blend until the chutney is well-mixed and resembles salsa.
• If you need to add water to reach the perfect consistency, then do so right at the end, a little at a time. On the other hand, if you find your chutney too runny, add a touch of gram flour or a few peanuts to soak up the liquid.

Coconut Chutney

(Serves 6)

Coconuts are an integral ingredient in Indian food. Their sweet flesh provides vital nutrients; the water helps to cool one down in the intense Indian heat; and the oil provides essential fats. However, coconut curries can be a little overpowering for those who are not used to the flavour. This chutney, often served with South Indian fare like Dhosa and Idli, allows you to introduce the fragrant, exotic, floral flavour, whilst affording diners control over the amount they add to their own meal.

INGREDIENTS

For the Chutney

150 g desiccated coconut
2 tsp ginger
3 green chillies
2 tbsp yoghurt
Salt to taste
½ tbsp sugar
10 g fresh coriander,
finely chopped

For the Fried Seasoning

2 tbsp sunflower oil
½ tsp mustard seeds
½ tsp fenugreek seeds
6 curry leaves
1 tsp urad daal (white lentils)

METHOD

• Combine the coconut, ginger, chillies, yoghurt, salt, sugar, and coriander in a food processor, and blend until the chillies are well chopped and blended with the other ingredients.
• Heat the oil in a small frying pan, and then add the mustard seeds, fenugreek seeds, curry leaves, and urad daal. Take care when doing this, as the spices will fizz and splutter a bit.
• Sauté the spices for a few seconds until the flavours have released into the oil – when it becomes really fragrant, you know it is ready.
• Add the seasoning to the yoghurt mixture in the food processor, and pulse to combine everything.
• Serve chilled.

Mint & Yoghurt Chutney

(Serves 4)

This light, cooling chutney is the perfect partner for hot and spicy foods. Not only does it freshen and cool the taste buds, the mint also helps to gently calm the stomach from all the fiery chillies. I love the contrast of hot and cool when serving this with dishes such as Chilli Paneer.

INGREDIENTS

50 g fresh mint
25 g fresh coriander
1 green chilli
1 tsp garlic
1 tbsp lemon juice
½ tbsp sugar
Salt to taste
2 tbsp yoghurt

METHOD

• Roughly chop the mint, coriander, and chilli, then place in a food processor along with the garlic.
• Blend all the ingredients together until well-combined.
• Add the lemon juice, sugar, and salt and blend again to create a vivid green salsa.
• Lastly, blend in the yoghurt. The result should be smooth, creamy, refreshing green chutney.

Mango Chutney

(Serves 6)

Mangoes are known as the national fruit of India and are consumed in many different forms – from fresh and ripe, to green and sour; in powdered form, and in drinks and desserts. The intensely orange, sweet, ripe mangoes are only in season for a few months, but their succulent flavour is unparalleled. This chutney allows you to preserve the bright, bold colour and flavour for a few months longer. It is a spicy relish, and you can always leave out the spices and make a sweet jam if you prefer. If you do so, I highly recommend mango and ginger. But, made to this recipe, this sticky, sweet sauce makes a divine dipping condiment, perfect with naan, paratha, or even poppadums.

INGREDIENTS

1 tbsp sunflower oil
½ tsp mustard seeds
2 green cardamom pods
2 cm cinnamon bark
1 tsp red chilli flakes
½ tsp minced garlic
½ tsp minced ginger
1 tsp coriander &
cumin powder
2 ripe mangoes, peeled
and diced
100 g soft brown sugar
60 ml distilled white vinegar
½ tsp salt

METHOD

• Heat the oil in a heavy-based saucepan until simmering hot, and then add the mustard seeds, cardamom pods, and cinnamon bark.
• As the whole spices begin to fizz and release their flavours into the oil, turn down the heat and add the chilli flakes, garlic, and ginger.
• Sauté this mixture for a few seconds before stirring in the coriander & cumin powder, followed by the mango, sugar, vinegar, and salt.
• Allow the chutney to stew gently over a low heat for about 30 minutes, stirring occasionally until the mango becomes 'mashable', and the chutney has reached a thick, syrupy consistency.
• Transfer to an airtight jar and allow to cool.
• Serve at room temperature, or store in the fridge and serve cold.

Date & Tamarind Chutney

(Serves 8)

My personal favourite, this dark, mysterious sauce is fruity, earthy, and wonderfully sweet and sour. It's perfect served with Samosas or Chaat. Dates grow in abundance in India and tamarind is a similar fruit, but much more sour in flavour. Dried varieties of both these fruits are quite easy to find in the U.K, and are great to keep in the store-cupboard for whipping up this chutney at short notice.

INGREDIENTS

250 g seedless dates
125 g dried tamarind
75 g jaggery or soft
brown sugar
200 ml water
1 tsp salt
2 tsp roasted ground cumin
(just dry-roast and grind
normal cumin seeds)
1 tsp minced ginger
¾ tsp red chilli powder

METHOD

• Roughly crumble the dates, tamarind, and jaggery into a saucepan.
• Add the water and place over a medium heat.
• Cook the mixture, stirring occasionally, until all of the ingredients have melted together and no lumps remain.
• Remove the saucepan from the heat and use the back of a spoon to press the mixture through a sieve and into a heatproof bowl. This will remove any skins or seeds that may have been left in the dates or tamarind.
• While the chutney is still warm, stir in the salt, cumin, ginger, and chilli.
• Allow the chutney to cool down completely before serving. If you find that it thickens too much while cooling, just stir in a little water.
• This chutney can be stored in the fridge for up to 2 weeks.

Baingan Raita

(Serves 6)

This yoghurt-based sauce was one of my Grandma's signature recipes. Instead of the popular cucumber Raita, she would blend smoky, roasted aubergine with creamy yoghurt and light spices to create this more unusual version. Not only is it delicious served with breads, rice dishes or Handwo, it is also a great way to incorporate nutritious aubergines in your diet.

INGREDIENTS

1 large ripe aubergine (about 200 – 250 g)
1 tsp sunflower oil
½ tbsp sugar
50 ml yoghurt
½ tsp red chilli powder
1 tsp ground roasted cumin
½ green chilli, finely chopped
15 g fresh coriander
Salt to taste
Lemon juice to taste

METHOD

• Preheat the grill to the highest heat. Prick the aubergine all over with a fork, rub with the oil, and place under the grill. Turn the aubergine every few minutes for a total of around 15 minutes or until the skin is charred on all sides.
• Remove from the heat and allow to cool slightly before gently peeling off and discarding the skin.
• Scoop the aubergine flesh into a mixing bowl, add all remaining ingredients apart from the lemon juice, and mix well.
• Taste the Raita for sharpness, and add a little lemon juice if you feel the yoghurt isn't quite tart enough. Serve chilled.

SNACKS & 'FARSAAN'

Everyone in my family loves savoury snacks and nibbles, also known as 'farsaan' .These are like the canapés of Indian food, bite-sized morsels that you can pick up and eat without the need for cutlery or plates. The term 'Farsaan' denotes light, flavourful side dishes which add lots of colour, texture, and interest to main meals. Served with chutneys and beautifully-presented, they make stunning eye candy - and taste even better than they appear.

Sambharo

(Serves 4)

A colourful, stir-fried salad, Sambharo is most often served as accompaniment to a main meal, but it also works well as a light starter, complimenting dishes such as Dhokra and Handwo too. It is sweet, sour, spicy... and very moreish.

INGREDIENTS

500 g cabbage
2 carrots
4 green chillies
2 tbsp sunflower oil
2 tsp mustard seeds
Salt to taste
¼ tsp turmeric
2 tbsp lemon juice
1 ½ tbsp sugar

METHOD

• Start by preparing the vegetables; coarsely grate the cabbage and thinly slice the carrots and chillies into 2.5 cm pieces.
• Heat the oil in a karahi or wok over a high heat, and then add the mustard seeds.
• When the mustard seeds begin to fizz, add the cabbage, carrots, and chillies, followed by the salt and turmeric.
• Stir-fry for a few minutes until al dente, and then add the sugar and lemon. Mix well to combine.
• When the sugar has fully dissolved and the vegetables are still crunchy, the Sambharo is ready to serve.
• This salad can be served either hot or at room temperature.

Bhindi Masala

(Serves 4)

Okra, or 'ladies' fingers', as they are commonly referred to, have gained a bit of a bad reputation - because quite often, they are not cooked correctly and become unpleasantly slimy. However, with the right preparation and a little spice, they can be transformed into this delicious, crisp and tangy side dish. Just take care to carefully wash and dry each stem and all should be well. Serve as an accompaniment to any main course with breads and rice– a great way to get kids to eat those greens!

INGREDIENTS

350 g bhindi (okra)
3 tbsp sunflower oil
1 ½ tsp cumin seeds
1 large onion, sliced
2 tsp crushed garlic
Salt to taste
2 tsp red chilli powder
½ tsp turmeric
2 tsp coriander &
cumin powder
2 tomatoes, sliced
1 ½ tbsp lemon juice

METHOD

• Start by thoroughly washing the okra and then scrupulously drying each one with kitchen paper.
• Top and tail the okra and chop them in half lengthwise.
• Add the oil to a wide frying pan placed over a medium heat. Once the oil is hot, add the cumin seeds.
• When the cumin seeds begin to fizz in the oil, add the onions and fry until they begin to brown.
• Stir in the garlic and sauté for about 30 seconds before adding the okra to the pan.
• Mix in the salt, chilli powder, turmeric, and coriander & cumin powder, then reduce the heat to low, cover the pan, and allow to cook for 5 minutes.
• Keep the okra covered as they cook, stirring occasionally until they begin to soften.
• When the okra is slightly soft, remove the lid from the pan, and increase the heat to medium-high.
• Add the tomatoes and lemon juice, mix well, and cook, stirring frequently until the okra are tender.
• Serve with hot chapattis.

Tip: To make a crispier version of this recipe, chop the okra in half and quickly shallow-fry in hot oil for a few minutes. Remove from the oil, drain on kitchen paper, and then proceed with the recipe as above.

Vegetable Samosas
(Serves 6)

Light, crisp pastry triangles filled with a sumptuous, tangy vegetable filling, Samosas are amongst the most well-known, best-loved Indian snacks. Served with an array of jewel-like chutneys, these golden parcels are tasty treasures that will always go down a treat. The 'folding' part of this recipe can be tricky at first, but you will get the hang of it after the first few - and the finished samosas are well worth the effort.

INGREDIENTS

For the Pastry

100 g plain flour, plus
1 tbsp extra
½ tsp salt
1 tsp lemon juice
50 ml warm water, plus
1 tbsp extra

For the Filling

1 large onion
1 large carrot
1 large potato
50 g peas
50 g sweetcorn
2 tbsp sunflower oil, plus
more for deep-frying
2 cloves
3 cm cinnamon bark,
roughly crushed
1 ½ tsp ginger
1 green chilli, finely chopped
2 tsp salt
¼ tsp turmeric
1 tsp chilli powder
1 tbsp lemon juice
½ tbsp sugar
Large pinch of chopped fresh
coriander leaves
(chopped roughly)

METHOD

• Begin by making the dough for the pastry. Place 100 g flour into a mixing bowl and stir in the salt and lemon juice.
• Add as much water required to knead the flour into soft, smooth dough that is moist, but not sticky. Leave aside to rest while you prepare the filling.
• Chop the onion, carrot, and potato into small, even cubes; roughly the same size as sweetcorn kernels.
• Heat 2 tbsp oil in a large pan, and when hot, add the cloves and cinnamon.
• When these begin to sizzle, add the onion and cook, stirring frequently.
• When the onion becomes translucent, add the ginger and chilli, then sauté for a few moments.
• Add the carrot, potato, peas, and sweetcorn to the pan, and stir in the salt, turmeric, and chilli powder. Cook until all the vegetables are tender but not mushy.
• Stir in the lemon juice and sugar, and cook for 3 more minutes before tossing in the coriander leaves.
• Leave the filling mixture aside to cool completely.
• In the meantime, make the pastry shells for the samosas. Segment the prepared dough into walnut-sized pieces, and then break each 'walnut' in half.
• Place a heavy skillet over a low heat to warm up.
• Roll two of the dough halves into circles with a diameter of roughly 9 cm. Lightly grease the surface of each one with oil, sprinkle with a little bit of flour, and then 'stick' the greased sides together.
• Roll the doubled-up circle of pastry into a much larger circle, approximately 25 cm in diameter, and then carefully place this onto the warm skillet and roast for a few seconds on each side, until the surface becomes just very slightly pink and bubbly.
• Remove the pastry from the skillet and place onto a damp tea towel.

• Use the tip of a long knife to pry the two circles apart, taking great care not to burn yourself. Cover with another damp tea towel to keep the pastry moist.
• Repeat the process with the remaining dough.
• When all the pastry is ready, cut it into halves or thirds, depending on how big you would like your finished samosas to be.
• Wait until both filling and pastry are completely cold and ready to handle.
• Make a 'glue' to hold the samosas together by mixing some flour and water to make a sticky paste.
• Lay a piece of pastry roasted side down and horizontally across your left palm (or right palm if you are left-handed).
• Bring the bottom left hand corner up and over the middle to create a straight vertical line down the centre of the pastry. Hold this in place with your thumb.
• Now spread a little of the 'glue paste' along the remaining bottom horizontal edge of the pastry and bring this up and over to meet the outer left edge – it will create a point at the bottom of the pastry. Press into place to secure.
• Turn the pastry over, so that you have an open cone facing you.
• Place a pea from the filling down into the point of the samosa. This will help provide a barrier just in case the pastry opens up when frying. Fill the cone three-quarters full with the stuffing.
• Spread a little of the paste on the top flaps of the pastry, then 'glue' them down onto the body to create neat little triangular parcels. Leave the filled samosas aside under a damp tea towel while you prepare the rest.
• Over a medium-high setting, heat enough oil in a wok or karahi to deep-fry the samosas.
• When the oil is ready, deep-fry the samosas until golden and crisp.
• Serve hot, at room temperature, or cold, with chutneys of your choice.

Tips: If you have any leftover filling, it makes a great filling for toasted sandwiches, or even simply served up with some chapattis the next day.

If you have leftover pastry, fry it and sprinkle with a few of your favourite spices. This makes a delicious snack similar to the one sold in many Indian shops and sweetmarts!

'Samosa Chaat' is an alternative way to serve – and a Mumbai street food favourite. Break the samosas into pieces; pile with date and tamarind chutney, mint chutneys and yogurt; add some sev (gram flour vermicelli); and serve in bowls.

Kachori

(Serves 6)

Often served alongside - or instead of – Samosas, these morsels of short, biscuit-like pastry are stuffed with a light pea and mint filling. The flavour is sweet and savoury, perfect when paired with date and tamarind chutney. When you bite in, the vibrant green filling looks stunning against the dark sauce.

INGREDIENTS

For the Pastry

100 g plain flour
½ tsp salt
2 tbsp sunflower oil
50 ml cold water

For the Filling

1 tbsp sunflower oil, plus more for deep-frying
½ tsp cumin seeds
¾ tsp ginger
1 green chilli
100 g peas
1 ½ tsp salt
½ tsp turmeric
1 tbsp lemon juice
½ tbsp sugar
1 tbsp desiccated coconut
Large pinch of finely chopped fresh mint
1 medium potato, boiled and peeled

METHOD

• Start by making the pastry dough. Put the flour in a mixing bowl and stir in the salt and oil. Add the water as required to form soft dough that's moist but not sticky. Leave aside to rest.
• Heat the oil in a pan placed over a medium heat. Add the cumin seeds and when they begin to fizz, add the ginger and finely chopped chilli.
• Sauté the ginger and chilli for a few moments, then add the peas, salt, and turmeric. Stir and cook until the peas become tender.
• Mix in the lemon juice, sugar, and coconut, and continue to cook for a further 5 minutes. Leave aside to cool.
• When the mixture is completely cool, add the mint. Mash in the boiled potato, roughly mashing the peas as you go.
• In a wok or karahi placed over a medium heat, heat sufficient oil to deep-fry the kachori.
• Take a cherry-sized segment of the dough and roll into a circle approximately 10 cm in diameter.
• Take 2 tbsp of the filling mixture and roll into a ball. Place the ball in the centre of the pastry circle.
• Bring the sides of the pastry up around the ball, gather the excess at the top and twist it off, taking care not to tear the sides of the pastry as you go. Gently roll the pastry-enclosed ball in your palms so that you have a smooth, round ball.
• Keep the fully-formed kachori from drying out by placing it under a damp tea towel while you prepare the rest.
• Deep-fry over a gentle heat until the pastry bubbles, becomes lightly golden, and is cooked through.
• Serve hot, with date and tamarind chutney.

Dhokra

(Serves 4)

Gujarati snack food at its best! People from the region are known to eat these light, yellow, savoury sponges at breakfast, lunch, and dinner. My Grandma used to make a slightly different version, where flour is soaked in sour yoghurt overnight to produce slightly denser, flatter slices of this cake-like snack, but this is the 'instant' version - ready in half an hour, producing great thick, fluffy wedges of savoury cake.

INGREDIENTS

For the Dhokra

350 g gram flour
2 tsp salt
2 tsp sugar
1 tsp ginger
1 finely chopped green chilli
1 ½ tsp citric acid OR 2 tbsp lemon juice
60 ml sunflower oil
550 ml water
Red chilli powder for sprinkling

For the Fried Seasoning

4 tbsp sunflower oil
2 tsp mustard seeds
Large pinch of curry leaves
1 tbsp sesame seeds
Large pinch of finely chopped fresh coriander

METHOD

• Prepare a steamer with water and place a snugly fitting, greased deep dish or cake tin inside the vessel. Place over a low heat.
• Sift the gram flour into a large mixing bowl and stir in the salt, sugar, ginger, and chilli.
• Add the citric acid or lemon juice, sunflower oil, and water, and whisk the mixture into a smooth batter.
• Pour the batter into the prepared dish inside the steamer, sprinkle a little red chilli powder over the top, and then quickly put the lid on.
• Increase the heat to medium-high, and allow the batter to steam for 15 minutes.
• After 15 minutes, turn off the heat, wait one minute, and then carefully remove the lid from the steamer.
• Transfer the cake tin or dish to a wire rack and allow the Dhokra to cool a little.
• Leave the Dhokra in the tin, but score into small pieces. Leave to rest whilst you prepare the seasoning.
• Heat the oil in a frying pan over a high heat, and then add the mustard seeds and curry leaves to the hot oil. Immediately reduce the heat to low and add the sesame seeds. When these have lightly coloured switch off the heat and add the coriander.
• Pour the seasoning over the scored Dhokra, allow it to soak in for a few minutes, and then gently cut and lift each piece of Dhokra onto a serving plate.
• Serve with lots of chutney.

Patra

(Serves 6)

These slices are the Indian equivalent of the popular Middle Eastern 'Dolma', stuffed vine leaves. They take a fair bit of preparation, but the finished green and gold roulades are beautiful and worth all the effort. It's not essential to add the fried seasoning, but it provides wonderful flavour and texture, giving the leaves a slightly smoky effect on the outside but leaving them soft and moist in the middle.

INGREDIENTS

For the Patra Leaves

24 colocasia leaves
100 g rice flour
700 g gram flour
2 tbsp ginger
2 tbsp garlic
3 finely chopped green chillies
3 tsp salt
1 tsp tamarind concentrate,
or add lemon juice for a
zesty flavour
100 g jaggery
Water for mixing

For the Fried Seasoning

3 tbsp oil
Small pinch of asafoetida
Large pinch of curry leaves
2 tsp minced garlic
50 g couscous
50 g sesame seeds
1 tsp salt
1 tsp red chilli powder

METHOD

• To prepare the leaves, carefully trim back any thick veins so that each leaf is as flat as possible – thick veins in the middle of the leaves will not cook through properly, so you need to try to make the leaves even.
• Lay each leaf on a flat surface one at a time, and carefully go over them with a rolling pin to make them perfectly flat and thin all over.
• Taking care not to tear the leaves, gently wash each one and leave to dry completely.
• When the leaves are dry, prepare the filling to spread over them. Sift the rice and gram flours into a large mixing bowl, add the ginger, garlic, chillies, salt, tamarind (or lemon juice), and jaggery, and stir to combine.
• Add the water and mix to form a thick, spreadable paste.
• Place one leaf on a flat surface, shiny side down with the point facing to your right.
• Use the fingers of one of your hands to spread some of the filling mixture all over the surface of the leaf.
• Using your clean hand, place a second leaf on top of the first, shiny side down with the point facing to your left, and again spread with more of the filling paste.
• Fold the top third of the pair of leaves over the middle third, and spread with a little more filling.
• Fold the bottom third of the leaves over the middle section so that you are left with one long, horizontal strip, and spread with even more filling.
• Fold approximately 2.5 cm of one side of the strip of leaves over to seal that end off. From that side, tightly roll up the leaves to form a taut roulade.
• Leave aside while you repeat the procedure with the remaining leaves.
• Prepare your steamer and place the stuffed leaves inside to steam for approximately one hour. You will know the leaves are cooked as they will change colour and appear softened.
• Allow the roulades to cool completely before slicing them into 1.25 cm rounds.
• Heat 3 tbsp oil for the seasoning in a wide, shallow pan set over a high heat.
• Add the curry leaves, asafoetida, couscous, and garlic to the hot oil.
• Carefully place the sliced stuffed leaves into the pan, and sprinkle over the sesame seeds, salt, and red chilli powder.
• Stir-fry, carefully turning the rolled leaves, until slightly browned.
• Serve hot.

Crispy Bhajia

(Serves 6)

Lightly-battered, super-crunchy, intensely-flavoured potato crisps – everyone adores these! These make a great starter, but my favourite way to enjoy them is alongside spiced popcorn while watching a classic Bollywood film. The combined aroma, taste and texture of the snacks just seem to bring the movie to life and transport me to an Indian movie theatre.

INGREDIENTS

250 g large white potatoes
75 g gram flour
50 g rice flour
25 g corn meal
2 tsp ginger
1 tsp garlic
1 tsp green chilli, finely chopped
1 tsp salt
½ tsp turmeric powder
1 tbsp yoghurt
½ tsp sea salt
½ tsp red chilli flakes (or powder)
10 g fresh coriander, finely chopped

METHOD

• Thinly slice the potatoes and place the slices in a mixing bowl.
• Sift the three different flours directly into the bowl, over the potatoes.
• Add the garlic, chilli, salt, and yoghurt, and mix well so that all of the potato slices are covered in a mixture of the flours and spices.
• Cover the bowl in cling film and leave in the fridge for 1 hour.
• When the hour is up, heat some oil for deep-frying the potatoes in a large wok.
• When the oil is ready, carefully add some of the potato slices and fry until golden and crisp.
• Drain on kitchen paper and check to make sure the potatoes are cooked through – if not, you may need to lower the heat of the oil slightly.
• Fry all the potato slices and sprinkle with the sea salt, red chilli flakes, and fresh coriander whilst still warm, for added texture and colour.
• Serve hot with lots of chutney.

Fulavra

(Serves 6)

The previous recipe for Crispy Bhajia can be adapted slightly to create an abundance of bhajia varieties including aubergine, onion, chillies, and paneer, but the recipe that follows is my Grandma's favourite of all. These small fried dumplings are crunchy on the outside and soft and moist on the inside. The inclusion of fenugreek leaves and grated carrot adds beautiful texture and flavour.

INGREDIENTS

50 g fenugreek leaves, chopped
160 g cooked rice
1 medium onion, finely chopped
½ carrot, coarsely grated
1 tbsp yoghurt
1 tsp garlic
1 tsp ginger
1 green chilli, finely chopped
1 tsp salt
¼ tsp turmeric
½ tsp red chilli powder
½ tsp carom seeds
Pinch of asafoetida
150 g gram flour
6 tbsp water
1 tsp fruit salts (such as Eno)
OR 1 ½ tsp bicarbonate of soda
Oil for deep-frying

METHOD

• Place the fenugreek, rice, onion, and carrot in a mixing bowl and add the yoghurt, garlic, ginger, green chilli, salt, chilli powder, carom seeds, and asafoetida.
• Sift in the gram flour and mix everything together really well before adding enough water to make a thick batter with a dropping consistency.
• Heat the oil for frying in a wok or karahi placed over a medium heat.
• When the oil is hot, very carefully place teaspoon-full amounts of batter into the oil, 3 or 4 at a time.
• Fry the batter until it puffs out into golden brown dumplings, and drain on kitchen paper.
• Serve hot with generous amounts of chutney.

Bateta Vada

(Serves 8)

Wonderfully soft, floury, spiced potatoes coated with a light, crisp gram flour batter; these spicy little treats are a real winner at dinner parties. Serve individually with a touch of chutney as canapés, or stack in a bowl for a moreish, tasty starter – either way, these beautifully golden morsels are sure to delight.

INGREDIENTS

For the Filling

500 g potatoes
2 tsp salt
1 tsp chilli flakes
½ tsp chilli powder
2 ½ tsp ginger
2 green chillies,
finely chopped
½ tsp turmeric
Juice of half a lemon
1 tbsp sugar
Small handful of fresh
coriander leaves,
finely chopped

For the Batter

150 g gram flour
1 tsp salt
½ tsp paprika
1 tbsp yoghurt
100 ml water
Large pinch of finely chopped
fresh coriander leaves
Sunflower oil for deep-frying

METHOD

• Boil or steam the potatoes until completely tender and leave aside to cool completely.
• Peel the potatoes, place the cooked flesh in a large mixing bowl, and mash until smooth.
• Add all of the remaining ingredients for the filling to the potatoes, and mix well until smooth and well-seasoned. Leave aside.
• To make the batter, sift the gram flour into a bowl, stir in the salt and paprika, and then whisk in the yoghurt and water until the batter has the consistency of pancake batter.
• Heat the oil for deep-frying in a wok or karahi placed over a medium-high setting.
• Take 2 tablespoons of the potato mixture at a time and roll into balls. When the oil is hot, use a long-handled spoon to dip and coat the potato balls in the batter, and then very carefully place them into the hot oil.
• Fry a few balls at a time, turning in the oil until they are golden all over.
• Drain on some kitchen paper and serve hot with chutneys and tea.

Khandvi

(Serves 6)

These little sweet-and-sour gram flour rolls look so pretty and are really quick and easy to make. Ensure you have plenty of surface area greased and ready to spread the hot batter on to – if you do not have a lot of counter top space, you can use the backs of trays, plates, or anything flat. If, for any reason, the Khandvi do not roll, just scrape the mixture back into the pan, add a little more water, re-heat, and try again.

INGREDIENTS

For the Khandvi

60 g gram flour
100 g yoghurt
125 ml water
1 tsp ginger
½ green chilli, finely chopped
½ tsp salt
½ tsp turmeric
½ tsp lemon juice

For the Fried Seasoning

1 tbsp sunflower oil
½ tsp mustard seeds
5 curry leaves
Pinch of finely chopped coriander
2 tsp sesame seeds
1 tbsp desiccated coconut

METHOD

• Start by lightly greasing your work surface or the backs of about 3 large steel trays – you will need to have these ready to use as soon as the mixture is cooked.
• Combine all of the ingredients for the Khandvi in a small saucepan and place over a low heat.
• Stir continuously over the heat until the mixture thickens to the point that it starts to come away from the pan as you stir.
• Turn off the heat and pour the mixture onto the prepared surfaces.
• Working as quickly as you can, use a palette knife to thinly spread the mixture in an even layer over the greased surfaces – you need to be fast, as the mixture will cool and become un-spreadable fairly quickly.
• Allow the mixture to cool for 1 minute before using your knife to score columns approximately 2.5 cm wide through the mixture.
• Wait a few more moments for the mixture to firm up before proceeding to the next step.
• Starting at the end of the first column, use your palette knife to assist you in gently lifting the set mixture away from the surface.
• Roll this up over itself until the roulade is around 2 cm thick. Cut the end and repeat with the remaining mixture.
• Arrange the little rolls on a serving plate.
• For the seasoning, heat the oil in a small frying pan, then add the mustard seeds and curry leaves.
• When these begin to fizz and pop, turn off the heat and add the coriander leaves and sesame seeds.
• Pour the seasoning over the Khandvi rolls and then sprinkle the desiccated coconut over the top.
• Serve as a snack with Masala Chai (recipe on p138).

Hara Bhara Kebabs
(Serves 12)

These vegetable fritters take their name from the beautiful emerald green hues of the key ingredients. Often found on restaurant menus, these kebabs are actually incredibly easy and quick to make at home, so they make a great speedy treat – especially at tea-time.

INGREDIENTS

750 g potatoes
200 g peas
250 g spinach
2 ½ tsp salt
2 tsp coriander &
cumin powder
3 tsp garlic
3 tsp ginger
4 green chillies, finely
chopped Juice of 1 lemon
2 tbsp sugar
Oil for shallow-frying

METHOD

• Boil or steam the potatoes and peas separately until completely tender. While they are cooking, allow the spinach to soak in freshly boiled water so that it cooks down a bit too.
• Strain all of the vegetables and allow them to cool completely.
• Peel the potatoes and combine with the peas and spinach in a large mixing bowl. Mash together until broken down and well-combined.
• Mix in all of the remaining ingredients until everything is really well combined. You should have a sort of mashed dough that holds together.
• Take a tablespoon of the mixture and roll it into a smooth ball, then flatten the ball and neaten up the edges to make a patty which is about 1cm thick.
• Repeat with all of the remaining mixture. Keep a bowl of water nearby and if you find that the patties stick to your hands, dampen your hands between forming each one.
• When all of the patties are ready, heat a tablespoon of oil in a wide, shallow frying pan placed over a medium-high heat.
• Place a few patties onto the hot pan. Don't put too many at once, or it will be difficult to lift and turn them. I normally do 4 at a time in a 25 cm pan.
• Fry on the first side for about 2 minutes, or until browned, and then carefully lift and turn each patty with a spatula. Fry the other side for the same amount of time.
• When the patties are cooked, allow them to drain for a few moments on a sheet of kitchen paper.
• Serve hot with chutney for dipping.

Tip: If you find that the potato mixture is too wet, or isn't holding together properly, add some gram flour to thicken it.

Handwo

(Serves 12)

This is a recipe for a spicy Indian 'cake' perfect for afternoon tea parties, picnics and barbecues. Handwo tastes best served alongside a cup of Masala Chai. It is best to soak the flour overnight, but if you do not have the time a few hours will do. Specially-blended Handwo flour can be purchased from most Indian grocery stores, but if you can't find it, use equal quantities of gram flour, split pigeon pea flour, white lentil flour, and rice flour.

INGREDIENTS

For the Handwo

600 g handwo flour (or the mixture described)
1 tsp salt
¼ tsp turmeric
300 g yoghurt
400 ml hot water
100 g fresh fenugreek, finely chopped
250 g bottle gourd (doodhi), grated
1 large carrot, grated
2 onions, grated
1 tbsp ginger
1 tbsp garlic
2 green chillies, finely chopped
2 tsp salt, extra

For the Fried Seasoning

50 ml sunflower oil
1 tsp mustard seeds
1 tsp cumin
10 curry leaves
¼ tsp asafoetida
2 tbsp sesame seeds
1 tbsp fruit salts, such as Eno OR bicarbonate of soda

METHOD

• Sift the flour into a large mixing bowl and whisk in the salt, turmeric, yoghurt, and water.
• Cover and leave overnight in a warm place.
• The next day, pre-heat oven to gas mark 4/180C/350F and grease 2 muffin tins (or your choice of dish or tin).
• Mix the fenugreek, bottle gourd, carrot, onions, ginger, garlic, chillies, and extra salt into the prepared batter.
• For the seasoning, heat the oil in a small frying pan.
• When the oil is hot, add the mustard seeds, cumin, curry leaves, and asafoetida. Allow the spices to sizzle in the oil for a few seconds before turning off the heat and stirring in the sesame seeds.
• Pour the seasoning into the Handwo batter and mix well.
• Add the fruit salts and quickly mix thoroughly before pouring the entire mixture into the prepared tins.
• Place the Handwo into the hot oven and bake for 1 hour, or until it's golden on top and a knife inserted into the middle comes out clean.
• When baked, place the Handwo on a wire rack to cool - but cover the top surface with a clean, damp tea towel. This will help ensure that the Handwo
• When the Handwo is at room temperature, run a palette knife around the edge to release it from the pan and serve individual 'muffins' or generously cut slices with cups of Masala Chai (recipe on page 138).

Khichi

(Serves 6)

Steamed rice flour never tasted so good! These little dumplings pack a big punch of flavour; creamy and spicy at the same time. They are deceptively filling, so a little goes a long way. Every time I make these, they remind me of my Aunt – because, for as long as I can remember, this has been her all-time favourite food.

INGREDIENTS

750 ml water
2 tsp salt
1 tsp bicarbonate of soda
1 tsp cumin
½ tsp carom seeds
5 cloves
¼ stick cinnamon bark, roughly crushed
400 g rice flour, sifted
2 tsp sesame seeds
4 green chillies, finely chopped

METHOD

- Add the water to a large, heavy-based pan and place over a medium heat.
- Add the salt, bicarbonate of soda, cumin seeds, carom seeds, cloves, and cinnamon to the water and bring to the boil.
- Simmer for 10 minutes.
- Stir in the rice flour, sesame seeds and chillies and continue to stir, cooking the mixture until it thickens to a dough which comes easily away from the pan.
- Turn off the heat and leave aside until the dough is cool enough to handle.
- Prepare a steamer and line its bowl with a muslin or cheesecloth.
- Take about 2 tablespoons of the dough at a time and shape into a smooth patty. Use the end of a teaspoon to make a hole in the middle so that it looks like a small doughnut. The hole will allow the dough to cook through evenly.
- Place the little 'doughnuts' into the steamer, and loosely cover with the outsides of the cloth.
- Place the lid on the steamer and cook over a medium heat for 45 minutes.
- Turn off the heat and allow the steam to dissipate before removing the lid.
- Allow the Khichi to cool slightly before serving.
- Serve warm, drizzled with oil and sprinkled with chilli flakes.

STARTERS & STREET FOOD

This chapter is dedicated to the tantalising 'street food' most famously served along the roadside in Mumbai. The flavours are hot, tangy, and spicy, and often complimented with many of the chutneys you'll find in the first chapter of this book. On the streets of India, you would traditionally receive a plate heaped high with your favourite treat - but the flavours of these dishes have become so popular they're now often served up as refined, sophisticated starters at home, too.

Dahi Vada

(Serves 6)

This yoghurt-based dish is perfect for serving at summer parties, or even at barbecues because of its cooling, calming flavours and textures. The fritters which go into the yoghurt are very similar to falafel fritters, but are made from split black-eyed peas. If the soaking procedure seems a bit lengthy, you could skip that stage and use tinned beans instead.

INGREDIENTS

For the Fritters

500 g split black-eyed peas
1 ½ tsp ginger
1 tsp green chilli, finely chopped
1 tsp salt
Oil for deep-frying

For the Yoghurt

2 kg plain yoghurt
1 tsp salt
1 tsp cumin, dry-roasted and ground
2 tsp red chilli powder
10 g fresh coriander, finely chopped

METHOD

• The night before making this dish, give the beans a rough wash and leave them to soak overnight in a large bowl filled with plenty of warm water.
• The following day, drain the water from the beans and wash thoroughly, removing any shells that may have come loose whilst soaking.
• Place the wet beans in a blender and grind into a thick paste. Do not add any extra water, or the batter will become too runny to fry.
• Pour the bean paste into a mixing bowl and stir in the ginger, chilli, and salt.
• Heat oil for deep-frying in a wok placed over a medium-high setting. Keep a tray lined with kitchen paper to hand along with a large bowl half-filled with warm water.
• When the oil is hot, fry tablespoon-full amounts of the batter into fritters. When done, allow to drain on the prepared tray while you add more batter to the frying pan.
• While the new batch of batter is frying, place the previously-fried vada into the warm water. Allowing the fritters to get saturated with water keeps them sponge-like so that they absorb the yoghurt topping really well, but still retain a good bite.
• When all of the batter has been fried, leave all the fritters in the water until cool enough to handle.
• In the meantime, prepare the yoghurt by whisking it with the salt and roasted cumin until smooth.
• Gently squeeze the water from the fritters and place them onto your serving dish, discarding the soaking water.
• Pour the yoghurt mixture over the fritters, and sprinkle with chilli powder and coriander.
• Allow to rest in the fridge until you are ready to serve.

> Tip: These fritters are also a great alternative to falafel – instead of soaking the fritters in water, allow them to drain on kitchen paper and stuff them into warm pitta bread along with salad and yoghurt chutney.

Paneer Tikka

(Serves 6)

Succulent chunks of paneer; crunchy, vibrant peppers; flavourful onions; and tomatoes marinated in lightly spiced yoghurt - all grilled to a smoky finish. This easy, crowd-pleasing starter can be made in moments, but the longer you leave the marinade, the better the depth of flavour will be. This recipe is great for barbecues, but tastes just as good cooked under a conventional grill. Serve with hot flatbreads and lots of chutney.

INGREDIENTS

500 g paneer
2 peppers, preferably different colours for the most beautiful effect
100 g cherry tomatoes
6 shallots (or use any onions chopped into chunks)
250 g yoghurt
Salt to taste
¼ tsp turmeric
1 tsp lemon juice
1 tsp red chilli powder
2 tsp coriander & cumin powder

METHOD

• Cut the paneer into large chunks, (approximately 2 cm square). Keeping the bite-sized pieces chunky will help them stay nice and moist on the inside when grilled. Place the pieces into a large mixing bowl.
• Chop the peppers into similar-sized pieces and add to the bowl along with the tomatoes and shallots (cut these in half if they are too large).
• In a separate bowl, mix together the yoghurt, salt, turmeric, lemon juice, chilli powder, and coriander & cumin powder.
• Pour the yoghurt mixture over the paneer and vegetables, and toss together until everything is well-combined.
• Cover with cling film and leave aside to marinade for anything between 30 minutes to overnight.
• When you are ready to grill the tikka, thread the paneer and vegetables onto skewers, drizzle on a little extra sauce, and grill, turning when needed until lightly-charred on all sides. If you do not have skewers, just tip the paneer and vegetables onto a grill pan or baking sheet and grill, drizzling on sauce and turning as required, until done.
• Serve immediately.

Chilli & Garlic Mushrooms

(Serves 6)

Mushrooms have never looked as appetising and vibrant as they do in this recipe! The colour and crunch from the peppers along with the zingy aromas perfectly complement the juicy -interior of the battered mushrooms, creating a great-textured dish bursting with flavour. To make things a little easier, you can fry the mushrooms in advance and then quickly sauté everything together just before serving. This recipe makes a wonderful starter or side dish, but it's even good accompanied simply by plain rice.

INGREDIENTS

For the Mushrooms

250 g button mushrooms
4 tbsp plain flour
2 tbsp cornflour
½ tsp ginger
½ tsp garlic
½ tbsp light soy sauce
¼ tsp salt
Water to make a thick batter
Oil for deep- frying

For the Masala

2 tbsp sunflower oil
1 tsp garlic
½ tsp ginger
3 green chillies, finely chopped
2 peppers, different colours
5 tbsp chopped tomatoes
2 tbsp soy sauce
Salt to taste
½ tbsp sugar
1 spring onion, finely chopped

METHOD

• Place the oil for deep-frying in a small frying pan and set over a medium heat.
• Clean and chop the mushrooms in half, leave aside.
• Prepare the batter by combining the flours in a small bowl with the ginger, garlic, soy sauce, and salt. Mix well and add enough water to make a thick batter for coating the mushrooms.
• Dip the mushroom halves in the batter, and fry until lightly golden. Drain on kitchen paper and leave aside.
• To make the masala for the mushrooms, heat the sunflower oil in a large pan, and then add the garlic, ginger, and chillies, followed by the peppers.
• Allow the peppers to fry and slightly change colour before adding the tomatoes, soy sauce, salt, and sugar.
• Mix everything together well, and cook the gravy until the oil begins to separate from the tomatoes. At this point, add the mushrooms, stir well, and cook, covered, for a further 5 minutes.
• Serve hot.

Indian Potato Salad

(Serves 6)

This beautiful potato salad, known as 'Ferar Shaak' in Gujarati, combines the warmth of ginger, green chillies and black pepper with perfectly-cooked, fluffy potatoes and heaps of cooling yoghurt. It is a delicious alternative to the Great British buffet favourite.

INGREDIENTS

3 tbsp sunflower oil
2 tsp cumin
7 curry leaves
20 g cashew nuts
10 g peanuts
2 tbsp ginger
3 green chillies, finely chopped
7 large white potatoes, diced into bite-sized chunks
2 tsp milled black pepper
2 tsp coarse sea salt
Yoghurt to serve

METHOD

• Heat oil in a large pan placed over a medium heat.
• When oil is hot, reduce the heat to medium and add the cumin and nuts. Allow the nuts to colour slightly before reducing the heat to medium and adding the ginger and chillies.
• Sauté for a few moments before adding the potatoes to the pan.
• Stir in the pepper and cook over a medium heat until the potatoes begin to soften slightly.
• Cover the pan and reduce the heat further. Allow the potatoes to cook, gently tossing them in the pan occasionally until they become crisp on the outside and tender in the middle.
• Sprinkle in the sea salt and serve with a generous amount of yoghurt.

Stuffed Green Peppers
(Serves 4)

This recipe is a favourite of my Dad's. He loves to eat these stuffed, slightly spicy green peppers alongside most of his meals, and I think they make a pretty canapé-style starter too - perfect for simply picking up and up and popping in your mouth. They may be small and look unassuming, but these morsels give a burst of flavour to rival the most complex dishes.

INGREDIENTS

For the Peppers

150 g green poblano peppers
75 ml sunflower oil
50 g gram flour
2 tsp coriander & cumin powder
Salt to taste
½ tsp turmeric
1 tbsp sesame seeds
2 tbsp desiccated coconut
3 tbsp ground peanuts
Juice of half a lemon
1 tbsp jaggery OR sugar
Large pinch of finely chopped fresh coriander

For the Fried Seasoning

1 tbsp sunflower oil
1 tsp mustard seeds

METHOD

• Prepare a steamer or pressure cooker ready for cooking the peppers once stuffed.
• Wash the peppers thoroughly, drain, and leave aside to dry while you prepare the stuffing.
• Heat the oil in a frying pan placed over a medium heat. Stir the gram flour into the hot oil.
• Allow the gram flour to cook for about 2 minutes before stirring in the salt, coriander & cumin powder, and turmeric.
• Cook for a further 30 seconds before adding the sesame seeds, desiccated coconut, and ground peanuts. Mix well.
• Stir in the lemon, jaggery, and coriander leaves; turn off the heat, and leave aside to cool.
• Prepare the peppers for stuffing by making an incision down the length of each one.
• Use a teaspoon to scoop out the seeds of the peppers, without forcing the incision to open too much.
• When the stuffing has cooled, use your fingers to stuff a small amount into each pepper – do not over-fill or they will burst when they cook. Add just enough to keep the incision open by approximately 3 mm.
• Place the stuffed peppers into the prepared steamer or pressure cooker and cook for about 5-7 minutes, until tender but still retaining a slight bite.
• Cool for at least 10 minutes (you can prepare up to this stage well in advance, and complete the recipe just before you need to serve).
• Heat the oil for the seasoning in a wide frying pan placed over a medium-high temperature.
• When the oil is hot, add the mustard seeds. When the seeds begin to pop, carefully add the peppers. Fry for a few seconds on each side until blistered and charred in places.
• Serve hot or at room temperature.

Roasted Chilli & Garlic Mogo
(Serves 6)

This recipe features my favourite hot and tangy Indian fast-food flavours and combines them with cassava – a staple root vegetable in East African cuisine. Cassava - or 'Mogo' as it is known amongst the East African community - has similar properties to potato, and can be cooked in many of the same ways. This is one of the most-loved party foods in our home. It can be prepared hours before serving and simply kept warm in the lower shelf of the oven, where it will crisp up beautifully.

INGREDIENTS

1 kg cassava, fresh or frozen
2 green chillies, finely chopped
1 ½ tsp ginger
2 tsp garlic
1 tbsp light soy sauce
2 tbsp chopped tomatoes
Salt to taste
150 ml sunflower oil
2 tbsp chilli flakes OR 2 tsp red chilli powder
Lemon juice, to serve

METHOD

• If using fresh cassava, start by thoroughly washing and then peeling it. Chop the roots into manageable sized chunks. If using frozen cassava, skip straight to the next step.
• Steam or boil the cassava until it is half cooked. Careful not to overcook- if it becomes completely tender, it will turn to mush as it roasts in the oven.
• Drain the cassava and, when cool enough to handle, chop it into wedges approximately 3 cm by 8 cm, removing any of the stringy core of the cassava as you go.
• Add the chillies, ginger, garlic, soy sauce, tomatoes, and salt to the cassava, and toss together until the wedges are well-coated.
• Cover with cling film and leave aside to marinade for at least 2 hours (or overnight in the fridge).
• Pre-heat oven to gas mark 9/232C/475F and pour the oil into a large roasting tin. Place the tin on the highest oven shelf to heat up.
• After 20 minutes, carefully remove the roasting tin from the oven and place it directly over a high heat on the hob.
• Very carefully, tip the marinated cassava into the hot oil.
• Allow the cassava to sear on one side for a minute, and then carefully turn the wedges in the pan, ensuring they are all well-basted in oil.
• Take the pan off the heat and return the cassava to the oven.
• Roast for 45 minutes, turning occasionally, until the cassava is crisp on the outside and tender in the middle.
• When cooked, carefully transfer the cassava to kitchen paper to drain.
• Serve hot, sprinkled with the chilli flakes and lemon juice.

Chilli Paneer

(Serves 6)

Chilli Paneer has become one of the most popular street foods in India and is also enjoyed in restaurants around the world. There are many different variations of this stir-fried recipe, which always includes hot, spicy, and tangy Far Eastern flavours. Here is my favourite quick, simple version, delivering maximum flavour with minimum effort. The lettuce wrap and mint chutney not only help to cool the heat from the hot chilli, but also make for artistic presentation. Add a cocktail stick to hold each wrap together, and you have fiery little canapés.

INGREDIENTS

500 g paneer
3 peppers (different colours work best)
3 red onions
5 green chillies
2 tomatoes
3 tbsp light soy sauce
100 ml chopped tomatoes
1 tbsp lemon juice
1 tsp salt
2 tsp sugar
2 tbsp garlic
2 tsp ginger
1 tbsp ghee
2 tbsp sunflower oil
Lettuce leaves and mint chutney to serve

METHOD

• Chop paneer into chips approximately 1 cm by 4 cm and place into a large mixing bowl.
• Slice the peppers, onions, chillies, and tomatoes and add them to the paneer.
• Pour the soy sauce, chopped tomatoes, and lemon juice over the paneer and vegetable mixture, then sprinkle in the salt, sugar, garlic, and ginger.
• Toss all of these ingredients together until the paneer and vegetables are well-coated in the marinade.
• Cover the bowl with cling film and leave aside for at least 2 hours or overnight for the flavours to develop.
• When you are ready to cook, heat the ghee and oil together in a large wok. When hot, add the marinated paneer and vegetables along with all of the sauce, and stir-fry over a medium-high setting until the vegetables are cooked and the paneer is golden and crispy in places.
• Serve hot, wrapped in flattened lettuce leaves and drizzled with mint chutney.

Tip: You can also serve the Chilli Paneer alone, or wrapped in any flatbread of your choice. Just lay the flatbread on a plate, add the paneer with some salad and lots of chutney, wrap, and go! This is a great packed lunch option as it can also be eaten cold.

Papdi Chaat
(Serves 6)

Mumbai street food at its finest, Papdi Chaat is a feast of different flavours and textures that somehow all manage to fit themselves into small mouthfuls of this delightfully easy-to-make dish. You can if you wish, buy all of the different components of this recipe from most large supermarkets, but they are so undemanding to make I highly recommend giving this from-scratch recipe a go. The only item I would suggest buying is the Sev – tiny, crisp strands of gram flour, full of crunch and spice – as this requires a bit more time and specialist equipment to make. The Papdi are like little fried biscuits which provide a great base for all the delicious chutneys, potatoes, and chickpeas piled on top, giving you something to really sink your teeth into.

INGREDIENTS

For the Papdi

300 g plain flour
3 tbsp sunflower oil
1 tsp salt
1 tsp carom seeds
100 ml warm water
Oil for deep-frying

For the Chaat

7 medium potatoes
2 x 400 g tins of chickpeas
1 tsp red chilli powder
Salt to taste, extra
1 large onion
1 packet of thin sev (crisp gram flour vermicelli)
Mint & coriander chutney, date & tamarind chutney, yoghurt and chilli chutney to serve

METHOD

• For the Papdi, sift the flour into a mixing bowl.
• Stir in the oil; add the salt and carom seeds, and just enough warm water to make smooth but firm dough. Allow to rest for 30 minutes.
• In the meantime, boil the potatoes until completely tender. Drain and leave aside to cool.
• Pour oil for deep-frying into a deep wok or karahi and place over a medium heat.
• Divide dough into manageable amounts and roll out on an oiled surface until 2 – 3 mm thick.
• Prick the dough all over with a fork and use a 6 cm cookie cutter to cut circles from it.
• Deep-fry the circles of pastry in medium-hot oil for around 3 minutes each, until crisp and pale gold.
• Continue until all the dough is fried. It is useful to have a pair of helping hands when doing this, meaning one person can roll and cut the Papdi, while the other fries them.
• Leave the Papdi aside to cool while you peel and chop the potatoes into 1 cm chunks.
• Drain and wash the chickpeas well, then combine with the potatoes. Sprinkle with salt and chilli powder.
• Finely dice the onion.
• Divide the room-temperature Papdi into serving bowls. Pile with the prepared chickpeas and potatoes, followed by generous lashings of chutney and sprinkles of raw onion and sev.

Pani Puri
(Serves 6)

Another popular street food is this alternative to Papdi Chaat – Pani Puri or Gol Gappe as they are most commonly known. These are crisp little balloons of pastry which you crack open and cram with creamy potatoes and chickpeas; top up with fragrant mint water; and garnish with chutneys, sev, and onions - even pomegranate seeds or blueberries. You then pop the entire pastry case into your mouth, all in one go. The result is an explosion of crunchy, creamy, spicy, tangy, refreshing textures and flavours that somehow perfectly fuse and keep you going back for more.

INGREDIENTS

For the Puri (pastry cases)
70 g fine semolina
1 tsp of salt
½ tsp baking powder
60 ml chilled sparkling water
4 tbsp plain flour
1 tsp sunflower oil, plus extra for deep-frying

For the Pani (mint water)

750 ml water
20 g fresh coriander
50 g fresh mint
2 green chillies
1 tbsp mango powder (amchur) OR lemon juice to taste
2 tsp cumin, dry-roasted and ground
1 tsp sugar
Salt to taste

For the Filling

7 potatoes
2 x 400 g tins chickpeas (you can use mung beans if you prefer)
Red chilli powder to taste
Salt to taste
1 red onion, finely chopped
Sev and pomegranate seeds for garnishing (optional)
Date and tamarind chutney OR yoghurt chutney to serve

METHOD

• Start by making the Puri. Place the semolina, salt, and baking powder into a bowl and cover with the cold water. Allow the semolina to soak for 2 minutes before sifting in the plain flour.
• Knead the dough for 10 minutes until it feels less sticky, then add the oil and knead for a further 5 minutes. The dough should feel soft and elastic.
• Cover and allow to rest in the fridge for 30 minutes.
• Prepare a wok or karahi with oil for deep-frying, and place over a medium heat to warm up. At the same time, pre-heat your oven to gas mark 2/150C/300F.
• Divide the dough into 4 segments, and roll out each one on a lightly floured surface until approximately 2 mm thick. Use a 5 cm cookie cutter to cut circles from the pastry, and deep-fry in the hot oil until puffed and lightly golden. Drain on kitchen paper and repeat until the dough is used up.
• When all the Puri are fried, place them on a baking sheet and into the warm oven for about 20 minutes (turn over after 10 minutes) to ensure they become really crisp. Cool on a wire rack.
• In the meantime, prepare the Pani by combining 100 ml of the water with the coriander, mint, and chillies in a blender. Blend until you achieve a smooth paste, then add the remaining ingredients and blend well so that all of the ingredients infuse well into the water.
• Cover and refrigerate to allow the water to chill and the flavours to infuse further.
• Peel and dice the potatoes, and boil together with the drained chickpeas until soft and tender.
• Drain and leave aside to cool completely.
• To serve, toss the chickpeas and potatoes in a little red chilli powder and salt and place in a serving bowl. Stack the Puris on a serving plate, and pour the water into small shot glasses or a jug.
• Arrange the chutneys and garnishes alongside the Puri platter, and allow your guests to help themselves in the following manner: crack through the top of a Puri; fill just over halfway with the chickpea and potato mixture; top with the mint Pani; garnish with onion, sev, pomegranate, and chutney; eat in one big bite!

Tips: If you prefer to serve the Pani without the 'bits', strain the liquid before serving.
If you wish, you can prepare all the individual parts up to the point of serving a day in advance.
You can crack open the Puris and fill them with the potato mixture in advance if you prefer, but add the mint water and chutneys at the very last minute, otherwise the Puris will go soggy and become difficult to manage.

Pav Bhaji

(Serves 6)

This roadside meal is pure comfort food – a perfectly spiced vegetable mash served hot alongside warm rolls that have been lightly fried on a tava. It is a light meal but at the same time heartening, and so full of flavour. I like to serve this with homemade mini bread rolls, like sliders, or with wholewheat seeded rolls for extra texture and flavour. The mash is like a vegetable stew or hot pot – add any, and every, vegetable you like. The more, the better!

INGREDIENTS

1 small cauliflower
2 carrots
50 g green beans
3 large tomatoes
100 g peas
100 g spinach
(Feel free to also use broccoli, squash, beetroot, potatoes, any leafy greens, and aubergines – any vegetables that will soften when cooked)
2 tbsp sunflower oil, plus extra for shallow frying
2 cloves
2 inches cinnamon bark, crushed
2 onions, finely diced
3 tsp ginger
2 tsp garlic
3 green chillies, finely chopped
1 tbsp coriander & cumin powder
½ tsp turmeric
Salt to taste
Bread rolls, halved
Fresh lemon and coriander to serve

METHOD

• Wash and roughly chop the cauliflower, carrots, green beans, and tomatoes, combine with prepared peas and spinach, and leave aside.
• Heat the oil in a large, heavy pan. When hot, add the cloves and cinnamon. Allow these to fizz in the oil for a few moments before adding the onion.
• Sauté the onion over a medium heat until soft and translucent, then add the ginger, garlic, and chillies and cook for a few more moments.
• Add all of the prepared vegetables to the pan along with approximately 150 ml water, and mix in the coriander & cumin powder, turmeric, and salt. When everything is well-combined, cover the pan and allow the Bhaji to cook over a medium low heat, stirring occasionally, for 1 hour, or until all of the vegetables are completely tender.
• Uncover the pan and use a potato masher to roughly mash the vegetables together. You don't want to puree it; just sort of 'smash' or crush everything.
• If the mixture seems too wet after it's crushed, just turn up the heat and cook off any excess liquid.
• Remove from the heat and leave aside to cool just a little.
• Heat up a tava or flat frying pan over a fairly high setting. Drizzle on a little oil and place half a roll (or rolls, depending on how big your pan is) onto the pan to fry, cut side down. When the first side is nicely browned and crispy on the edges, drizzle some more oil on the top side of the roll, and flip.
• Sprinkle some fresh coriander on top of the Bhaji and serve warm alongside the hot, golden, Pav (bread rolls), with wedges of lemon for seasoning.

Ragra Pettis

(Serves 4)

This famous Indian street food item is more of a light meal than quick snack – Ragra refers to the spicy curry made using dried white peas, and the Pettis are fried potato patties which soak up the liquid from the curry; adding more texture, weight, and flavour to the dish. Although the Ragra is traditionally made with dried white peas which are soaked before cooking, you can substitute with frozen green peas or even tinned chickpeas if you aren't able to find them, or are short on time.

INGREDIENTS

For the Ragra

100 g dried white peas
2 tbsp sunflower oil
1 tsp cumin
2 cloves
2 cm cinnamon bark, crushed
1 tsp ginger
3 green chillies, two finely chopped
1 large onion, finely chopped
60 ml chopped tomatoes
½ tsp turmeric
2 tsp coriander & cumin powder
Salt to taste
1 tsp tamarind concentrate
10 g jaggery OR 2 tsp sugar

For the Pettis

4 large potatoes, boiled, peeled, and mashed
1 tbsp cornflour
Salt to taste
½ tsp turmeric
2 tsp ginger
1 green chilli, finely chopped
1 tbsp lemon juice
2 tsp sugar
20 g fresh coriander, finely chopped
Oil for shallow-frying
Date & tamarind chutney, coriander chutney, and sev to serve

METHOD

• The night before making this recipe, thoroughly wash the dried peas until the water runs completely clear. Leave to soak overnight in 1 L of warm water.
• The following day, when you are ready to cook, heat the oil in a large, heavy-based pan or a pressure cooker.
• When hot, add the cumin seeds. When they start to fizz, add the cloves and cinnamon.
• Add the ginger and the two finely chopped green chillies. Let the mixture sauté for a few moments before adding the chopped onion.
• Gently fry the onion until it becomes transparent before pouring in the chopped tomatoes, turmeric, and coriander & cumin powder. Cook until you see the oil start to separate from the tomatoes.
• Pour the soaked peas, along with their soaking water and the remaining chilli (pricked with a fork), into the pan, and stir well to combine everything. Allow to cook for approximately 30 minutes in a pressure cooker, or covered in a heavy pan, until the peas are completely tender and mushy.
• Take the lid off the pan (wait for the steam to dissipate first if using a pressure cooker), and stir in the salt, jaggery, and lemon juice. Add a little more water if you feel the peas are too dry, and then simmer for 5 minutes over a medium heat. Leave aside while preparing the Pettis.
• Combine all of the ingredients for the Pettis apart from the oil in a large mixing bowl, and knead everything together until well-combined.
• Using wet hands, shape the mixture into smooth balls approximately the size of a golf ball, and then flatten them into thick patties.
• Heat some oil for shallow-frying the patties in a flat-based frying pan.
• When the oil is hot, fry the patties on both sides until golden brown all over. Drain on kitchen paper.
• To serve, re-heat the Ragra if necessary, arrange the hot Pettis on a serving plate, and pour the warm Ragra on top. Garnish with chutneys and sev, and serve hot.

MAIN COURSES

They say home is where the heart is. That's particularly true of the recipes in this section. All of these recipes are dishes that I've grown up eating at our family home, and they're very dear to me. You can make a large portion of most of these and eat them with rice, or do it the traditional way by serving one vegetable dish and one of the lentil recipes alongside flatbreads, rice and lassi for a well-balanced, unforgettable Indian meal.

Stuffed Vegetable Curry

(Serves 6)

This recipe, more commonly known as 'Bharelu Shaak' or 'Akhu Shaak', is an advanced version of the stuffed chillies presented earlier in the book, this time with the inclusion of more vegetables and lots more of the delicious, spicy stuffing. The whole baby vegetables make for beautiful presentation. The key is to add the vegetables to the pan at specific moments, so that they all cook through perfectly without becoming mushy.

INGREDIENTS

For the Stuffing (masala)

5 tbsp sunflower oil
50 g gram flour
¼ tsp turmeric
1 tsp red chilli powder
2 tbsp coriander & cumin powder
2 tbsp coarsely ground peanuts
2 tsp garlic
1 tsp ginger
1 green chilli, finely chopped
1 tbsp desiccated coconut
1 tsp sesame seeds
Salt to taste
20 g fresh fenugreek, finely chopped
10 g fresh coriander, finely chopped
2 tsp lemon juice
1 tbsp jaggery OR sugar

For the Vegetables

8 baby aubergines
5 shallots
6 green poblano peppers
15 small new potatoes

For the Fried Seasoning

3 tbsp sunflower oil
½ tsp cumin
½ tsp mustard seeds
4 tbsp chopped tomatoes
125 ml water

METHOD

• Begin by preparing the masala stuffing. Heat the oil in a flat, heavy-based pan placed over a low temperature. When the oil is warm, stir in the gram flour.
• Add the turmeric, chilli powder, and coriander & cumin powder, then mix in the peanuts, garlic, ginger, chilli, coconut, sesame seeds, and salt.
• Keep stirring the mixture over a low heat until the nuts and spices begin to release an earthy, roasted aroma.
• Add the fenugreek and coriander and continue to stir until they combine with the stuffing and any excess liquid they release evaporates.
• Turn off the heat and stir in the lemon juice and jaggery. Leave the stuffing aside to cool.
• In the meantime, prepare the vegetables. Thoroughly wash and dry them, then take the aubergines and make crossways incisions in the base, going up two-thirds of the way to the top of the vegetables.
• Take the cleaned potatoes and make crossways incisions going from the bottom about two-thirds of the way along the length.
• Peel the shallots, remove the hard core at the bottom, and make the same incisions in these.
• Make incisions from the top to just above the tail of the chillies, and scoop out the seeds from inside.
• Carefully prising open the incisions in the vegetables, stuff the masala into each one – do not overfill them, or they will burst during cooking. Leave the stuffed vegetables aside while you prepare the seasoning, retaining any leftover masala.
• Heat the oil for the seasoning in a large, heavy pan big enough to fit all of the prepared vegetables inside, preferably in an even layer on the base.
• Add the cumin and mustard seeds to hot oil, adding the tomatoes when the seeds begin to fizz.
• Cook until the oil starts to separate from the tomatoes, and then carefully add the stuffed potatoes – dotting them around the pan so that you can place the other vegetables in between later.
• Drizzle in half of the water, and then cover the pan and allow the potatoes to cook over a medium-low heat for 7 minutes, or until just soft on the outside, turning occasionally if necessary.
• Add the aubergines in between the potatoes, pour in the rest of the water, cover, and continue to cook, stirring as and when you need to, until the potatoes and aubergines are half-cooked, about 5 more minutes.
• Now add the chillies and onions, and sprinkle in any remaining masala. Cover and cook, stirring as required, until the vegetables are tender (allow them to become a little crispy and charred at the bottom for extra flavour).
• Serve hot with flatbreads or plain rice.

Tips: This recipe is normally quite dry, but if you prefer to have more of gravy, just dissolve the leftover masala in as much hot water as you like and stir into the pan along with the chillies and onions. Take care when stirring, as you need to be as gentle as possible to stop the whole vegetables from falling apart.
You can, if you wish, cook this recipe in the oven at around gas mark 5/190C/375F – just make the seasoning and gravy in a large roasting pan and add the vegetables in the same way as above, tossing them in the gravy as and when required.

Undhiyu
(Serves 6)

This vegetable curry is like the Gujarati version of the more common Jalfrezi. You can use any combination of vegetables and even some of your favourite pulses to create this recipe; however the stars of the dish are the fenugreek dumplings that steam in the pan while the curry cooks.

INGREDIENTS

3 tbsp sunflower oil
½ tsp mustard seeds
½ tsp carom seeds
1 x 400 g tin kala channa (dark chick peas), washed and drained
250 g valor (Indian/hyacinth beans) OR any green beans, topped, tailed, and chopped into 2.5 cm pieces
4 medium potatoes, peeled and diced
1 medium aubergine, dice just before required
½ tsp turmeric
3 tsp coriander & cumin powder
½ tsp red chilli powder
2 tsp garlic
Salt to taste

For the dumplings

50 g gram flour
100 g cooked rice
½ tsp garlic
Pinch of turmeric
1 tsp salt
1 tbsp oil
25 g chopped fenugreek
300 ml chopped tomatoes
1 tbsp sugar

METHOD

• Heat up the oil in a large, heavy pan over a medium heat. When the oil becomes hot add the mustard and carom seeds and wait for them to begin to fizz and splutter.
• Add the dark chickpeas, valor, and potatoes to the pan, and stir in the turmeric, coriander & cumin powder, chilli powder, garlic, and salt.
• Cover the pan with a steel tray, and add 125 ml cold water to the tray. The heat created inside the pan will condense when it hits the cold tray above, allowing the flavours of the spices to concentrate within the pan whilst also helping the vegetables to cook a little quicker.
• When the water on top becomes hot, just stir it into the pan and leave the curry to cook, covered, stirring occasionally. If you do not have a tray, just add the cold water to the pan and cover it with the lid, then continue to cook and stir occasionally.
• While the curry cooks, prepare the mixture for the dumplings by combining all of the ingredients in a bowl and mixing them together well. Add a little water if the mixture appears too dry, and roll into grape-sized balls.
• When the valor, potatoes, and chickpeas are half-cooked, stir in the diced aubergine, and then dot the dumplings around the pan on top of the vegetables. Cover the pan and allow everything to cook through completely, stirring occasionally.
• When all the vegetables and the dumplings are cooked, carefully stir in the tomatoes and sugar, and simmer for 2 minutes.
• Serve hot with warm rotis.

Cholle

(Serves 8)

This popular spicy curry is one of my personal favourites. White chickpeas cooked until soft in piquant tomato gravy, served with rice and parathas – simple, delicious Indian soul food. I use a mixture of oil and ghee in this recipe simply to get the flavour of the ghee without overpowering the dish. This isn't the most traditional version of the recipe, which usually includes garam masala and sometimes even tea leaves to intensify the flavour. This is simply my favourite version passed down to me by my Mum - clean, tangy and highly-spiced.

INGREDIENTS

1 tbsp sunflower oil
1 tbsp ghee
1 tsp cumin
3 medium onions, finely diced
2 tsp ginger
3 tsp garlic
4 green chillies, finely chopped
100 ml chopped tomatoes
2 tsp coriander & cumin powder
Salt to taste
3 x 400 g tins of white chickpeas
1 large potato, diced
1 tbsp jaggery
1 tsp tamarind concentrate OR mango powder (amchur) OR lemon juice
Freshly-chopped coriander to garnish

METHOD

• Heat the oil and ghee together in a heavy-based pan over a medium-high temperature. When hot, add the cumin seeds.
• When the cumin seeds begin to fizz, add the onions and sauté until they become light brown.
• Stir in the ginger, garlic, and chillies, and sauté with the onions for a few moments to release the flavours.
• Pour in the tomatoes, and then add the coriander & cumin powder and salt. Cook, stirring occasionally, until you see the tomatoes and oil begin to separate from each other.
• Add the washed and drained chickpeas and diced potatoes to the pan, and mix well with the tomatoes.
• Cover the pan with a steel tray, reduce the heat to medium, and pour 150 ml cold water into the tray to help the flavours concentrate better in the pan and slightly quicken the cooking time. When the water becomes hot, stir it into the pan.
• Repeat the process until you have enough water in the pan to create runny gravy for the vegetables. (If you do not have a suitable tray, just pour 150 ml cold water at a time into the pan, stir, and cover with a regular lid. When the water in the pan becomes hot, add more cold water until you reach the right consistency).
• Cook slowly until the potatoes are tender and the chickpeas have become soft and creamy.
• Take the lid off the pan and stir in the jaggery and tamarind. Simmer for 5 more minutes, garnish with fresh coriander, and serve hot.

Corn & Coconut Malai Curry

(Serves 6)

This mild, coconut-flavoured curry makes a perfect light summer meal and is especially enjoyed by children. The corn is left on the cob which looks beautiful, although makes it a little messy to eat - but that's half the fun of it! The other half of the fun is had by mopping up the delicious gravy with naan, making sure nothing goes to waste. Malai curries are normally quite mild and creamy, which is why I like to pair them with coconut, adding a new dimension of flavour so you don't miss the more pungent spices.

INGREDIENTS

4 tbsp sunflower oil
1 tsp cumin
½ tsp fennel seeds
2 medium onions,
finely sliced
2 tbsp ginger
1 tbsp garlic
200 ml chopped tomatoes
¼ tsp turmeric
1 tsp red chilli powder
2 tsp coriander &
cumin powder
3 whole cobs of fresh corn,
sliced into 2.5 cm circles
1 x 285 g tin sweetcorn,
washed and drained
2 green chillies, pricked
all over with a fork
Salt to taste
3 tbsp yoghurt
1 x 400 ml tin coconut milk
20 g fresh fenugreek,
finely chopped
15 g fresh coriander to garnish

METHOD

• Heat the oil in a heavy-based pan or pressure cooker set over a medium heat. When hot, add the cumin followed by the fennel, and wait until they begin to fizz.
• Add the onions and sauté until they become transparent. Quickly add in the ginger and garlic and fry for a few moments before stirring in the tomatoes.
• Mix the turmeric, chilli powder, and coriander & cumin powder into the tomatoes, and cook over a medium heat until the oil and tomatoes visibly separate from one another.
• Add the sliced and loose corn, and mix well so that it all becomes coated in the tomato mixture.
• Pour in about 200 ml water, or just enough to cover the corn in the pan by 2 cm. Stir in the chillies and salt, cover, and leave to cook until the corn becomes tender – in a pressure cooker this will take approximately 30 minutes.
• When the corn is cooked stir in the yoghurt, coconut milk, and fenugreek, and simmer for 7 more minutes.
• Garnish with fresh coriander and serve hot with rice and warm naan.

Vegetable Manchurian

(Serves 6)

This type of tangy, spicy curry is often referred to as 'Indo – Chinese', and has become quite popular in Indian restaurants around London since the late 1990's. The flavours are quite clean, influenced by Southeast Asian cuisine. The gravy in this particular recipe is more like the clear broth more commonly featured in Oriental cuisine, rather than the thick tomato-based gravies usually associated with Indian food. There are many varieties of Manchurian curries, from gobi (cauliflower) to mushroom. This one, incorporating dumplings made from cabbage and carrot, is my favourite.

INGREDIENTS

For the Dumplings

1 vegetable stock cube
600 g cabbage
300 g carrots
5 tbsp plain flour
5 tbsp corn flour
2 tsp ginger
2 tsp garlic
1 green chilli, finely chopped
1 tbsp light soy sauce
1 tsp red chilli flakes
OR powder
Ground black pepper to taste
Salt to taste
Oil for deep-frying

For the Gravy

3 tbsp arrowroot or cornflour
2 tbsp oil
250 g spring onions
1 tbsp ginger
1 tbsp garlic
2 green chillies, finely chopped
3 tbsp light soy sauce
5 tbsp chopped tomatoes
1 tbsp balsamic vinegar
2 tbsp jaggery OR sugar
Salt to taste
10 g fresh coriander,
finely chopped

METHOD

- Dissolve the stock cube in 500 ml hot water and leave aside to cool.
- Finely chop the cabbage and coarsely grate the carrot.
- Combine the vegetables and stir in the flours, ginger, garlic, chilli, soy sauce, chilli flakes, pepper and salt.
- Mix well to combine. You should be able to take a tablespoon of the mixture and squash it into a rough ball that holds together. If this does not work, add a little more plain flour and some of the vegetable stock mixture until you achieve the right consistency. (You should still have about 400 ml stock left over for the gravy).
- Heat the oil in a karahi or wok placed over a medium-high temperature. The oil is ready if you drop in some of the cabbage mixture in and it rises to the surface immediately.
- Take tablespoons of the cabbage mixture, roll into rough balls, and deep-fry until golden brown all over.
- Drain on kitchen paper and keep warm.
- Mix the arrowroot for the gravy into about 100 ml of the cold vegetable stock and leave aside.
- Heat the oil in a large pan, and then add the spring onions, ginger, garlic and chillies.
- Allow to cook until the mixture is lightly browned and has released its flavours.
- Carefully pour the remaining vegetable stock into the pan and stir well.
- Allow the stock to come to a boil over a high heat. Reduce the heat slightly before adding the soy sauce, tomatoes, vinegar, jaggery and salt.
- Mix well, and allow the sauce to come to the boil once more over a medium heat.
- Stir in the arrowroot mixture, and cook until the gravy thickens slightly.
- Arrange the dumplings in a serving dish and pour the gravy on top.
- Sprinkle with coriander and serve hot with rice.

Tip: If preparing this recipe ahead of time, keep the components ready separately until the last minute. To serve, warm through the stock, add the arrowroot, heat the dumplings, and then pour over the gravy. If you attempt to reheat the dish, the arrowroot causes the gravy to thicken, and the dumplings will become a mushy mess.

Aloo Gobi

(Serves 6)

This popular cauliflower and potato recipe is a mild, dry curry, similar to a stir-fry, and is great served with rice. The dish hails from Northern India, and is served in various styles all the way from Gujarat and Punjab to Nepal and Bangladesh. My version is taken from the stripped-back Gujarati recipe which uses minimal spices. Other versions use everything from garam masala and dried mango powder to yoghurt and onions – experiment and find your favourite way to enjoy this classic dish.

INGREDIENTS

2 tbsp sunflower oil
1 tsp mustard seeds
½ tsp cumin
½ tsp fenugreek seeds OR add
25 g finely chopped fresh
fenugreek when adding
the peas
1 medium cauliflower, cut into
small florets
2 medium potatoes, peeled and
diced into large chunks
2 tsp ginger
1 green chilli, finely chopped
2 tsp coriander & cumin
powder
1 tsp red chilli powder
½ tsp turmeric
Salt to taste
50 g peas
2 medium tomatoes,
roughly chopped
½ tbsp sugar
½ tbsp lemon
Fresh coriander to garnish

METHOD

• Heat the oil in a heavy-based pan over a medium-high setting. When hot, add the mustard seeds, cumin, and fenugreek seeds.
• When the seeds begin to fizz and pop, stir in the cauliflower, potatoes, ginger and chilli. Mix well and allow to sauté for 2 minutes, stirring constantly so that the ginger and chillies cook and release their flavours without burning.
• Reduce the heat to medium and stir in the coriander & cumin powder, chilli powder, turmeric, and salt.
• Cover the pan and allow the vegetables to cook for 7 – 10 minutes, until the potatoes are half-cooked.
• Mix the peas into the pan, cover again and allow to cook until the vegetables are all tender.
• Add the tomatoes, sugar, and lemon, toss everything together well, and cook for 3 more minutes.
• Sprinkle with coriander and serve hot with rice or naan.

Spinach & Corn Kofta Biryani

(Serves 6)

Biryanis are stunning, majestic rice dishes which are layered with thick, intense curried vegetables and finished with regal touches such as saffron, dried fruits, and nuts. They have a notorious reputation for being difficult and time-consuming to prepare. However, although the procedure is somewhat lengthy, this recipe for my vegetarian biryani is fairly straight forward and well-worth the time invested. The great thing is that other than some chutney which is entirely optional, this dish is a complete one-pot meal.

INGREDIENTS

For the Kofta

2 tsp sunflower oil
150 g spinach, roughly chopped
1 ½ tsp garlic
1 ½ tsp ginger
1 green chilli, finely chopped
2 medium potatoes, boiled
150 g paneer, crumbled
Salt to taste
1 ½ tbsp sugar
2 tbsp lemon juice
50 g coarse cornmeal

For the Sweetcorn Gravy

2 tbsp sunflower oil
1 tsp mustard seeds
1 tsp cumin
2 large onions, pureed
1 ½ tsp garlic
2 tsp ginger
1 green chilli, finely chopped
500 ml chopped tomatoes
Salt to taste
2 tsp coriander & cumin powder
½ tsp red chilli powder
¼ tsp turmeric
150 g sweetcorn
1 tbsp lemon juice
½ tbsp sugar

For the Rice

400 g long grain Basmati rice
1 ½ tsp sunflower oil
1 ½ tsp ghee
2 tsp cumin seeds
2.5 cm cinnamon bark, crushed
3 cloves
2 medium onions, finely chopped
200 g diced mixed peppers
Salt to taste

For the Fried Seasoning

100 ml sunflower oil
10 curry leaves
3 tbsp cashew nuts
3 tbsp peanuts
2 tbsp sesame seeds

METHOD

• Start by preparing the koftas. Heat the oil in a pan over a medium heat and add the spinach, garlic, ginger and chilli. Cook, stirring occasionally, for about 3 minutes, until the spinach is wilted and the flavours are well-combined. Leave aside to cool completely.
• Pre-heat oven to gas mark 9/240C/475F and grease a baking sheet.
• Combine the cooled boiled potatoes, paneer and room-temperature spinach together with all of the remaining ingredients for the kofta apart from the cornmeal, and mash together until well -combined.
• Add the cornmeal as required to form soft dough that doesn't stick to the bowl.
• Take one teaspoon of the mixture at a time and roll into smooth balls.
• Dust each ball in a little more cornmeal, place on the greased baking sheet and bake for about 20 minutes, turning occasionally, until browned.
• To make the gravy, heat the oil in a heavy-based pan placed over a medium heat.
• When the oil is hot, add the mustard and cumin seeds, and allow them to fizz in the hot oil, then add the pureed onion and cook over a low heat until the onions are light brown.
• Add the garlic, ginger, and chilli and allow them to sauté alongside the onions for a few moments.
• Stir in the tomatoes and add the salt, coriander cumin powder, chilli powder, and turmeric.
• Cook for a few minutes until you see the oil start to separate from the tomatoes.
• Add the sweetcorn, cover, and cook over a low heat until the sweetcorn is tender.
• Stir in the lemon and sugar, and then turn off the heat.
• Rinse the rice until the water runs clear and then soak it in clean water for one hour.
• Heat the oil and ghee in a large heavy-based pan. When hot, add the cumin, cinnamon, and cloves and allow to fizz.
• Add the onions and cook gently until they become translucent.
• Stir in the peppers.
• Drain the water from the rice and add the grain to the pan. Stir to ensure that all the grains of rice are lightly coated in oil.
• Pour in 1 L water, stir in the salt, cover the pan, and allow to cook over a medium heat, stirring very occasionally, for 20 minutes, or until the rice is al dente.
• Lower the heat of the oven to gas mark 5/190C/375F and lightly grease a large baking dish (transparent ones work beautifully as they allow the layers to show through).
• Press half of the rice (you don't have to wait for it to cool) into the bottom of the dish.
• Arrange the spinach kofta on top of the rice, and pour on the gravy and spread to make an even layer.
• Press the remaining rice on top.
• Prepare the seasoning by heating the oil in a small frying pan and adding the curry leaves, cashew nuts, and peanuts.
• Fry for 5 seconds before turning off the heat and adding the sesame seeds. Allow these to cook in the hot oil until browned.
• Pour the seasoning mixture on top of the biryani.
• Cover the biryani in foil and bake for 30 minutes.
• Allow to rest for 10 minutes before serving with chutneys of your choice.

Tadka Daal

(Serves 6)

This wonderful, sunshine-hued classic is a staple dish of Indian cuisine. The choice of Daal – the particular variety of lentil used in this curry - will vary across different regions, and in some cases mixed lentils are used. The 'Tadka' refers to the spiced, fried seasoning that is added to the slow-cooked lentils to not only provide flavour, but also cool the body and aid digestion. This recipe uses 'urad daal', which are white lentils (also confusingly known as split black lentils), as the main ingredient, with a handful of channa daal (split yellow gram) thrown in for texture. Use any variety of lentils you like and, if you opt for tinned over dried, you can even skip the soaking process.

INGREDIENTS

For the Daal

240 g dried urad daal (split black lentils)
30 g dried channa daal (split yellow gram)
1 tsp sunflower oil
¼ tsp turmeric
½ tbsp ginger
1 green chilli

For the Fried Seasoning

2 tbsp sunflower oil
½ tsp cumin
½ tsp nigella seeds
200 ml chopped tomatoes
2 tsp garlic
½ tbsp ginger
1 green chilli, finely chopped
¼ tsp turmeric
2 tsp coriander &
cumin powder
1 tsp red chilli powder
Salt to taste
Fresh coriander to garnish

METHOD

• The night before you are going to make the daal, measure the dry lentils out into the large pan or (preferably) pressure cooker that you intend on cooking them in. Very thoroughly wash the daal in warm water until it runs clear, and then leave to soak overnight (or at least 8 hours) in 750 ml warm water.
• When you are ready to cook the daal, place the pan, uncovered, over a high heat and bring to the boil. Some scum will rise to the surface, and you need to skim this off and discard it to make the lentils easier to digest.
• When the scum has been cleared, add the oil, turmeric, ginger, and chilli (having pricked it all over with a fork), stir well, cover, and cook for about 40 minutes or until the daal is tender – watch out for the channa daal, as it may require a little more time than the urad daal.
• After the lentils have cooked through, leave them to simmer, uncovered, over a low heat while you prepare the Tadka.
• For the Tadka, heat the oil in a small frying pan over a medium-high heat, and then add the cumin and nigella seeds.
• When the seeds begin to fizz, reduce the heat slightly and add the tomatoes. Stir in the garlic, ginger, chilli, turmeric, coriander & cumin powder, chilli powder, and salt. Cook the mixture until the oil and tomatoes begin to separate from each other.
• Turn off the heat and carefully pour the Tadka into the simmering daal. Mix well and bring to the boil.
• Simmer over a medium heat for 5 minutes and then serve hot, garnished with fresh coriander, alongside some plain rice.

Daal Makhani

(Serves 6)

This dark, earthy Daal is another firm favourite in our family. It is so simple, wholesome, and delicious – comfort food, if you will. Everybody who makes it has their own unique version but it's almost impossible to get wrong. My Dad's is usually the most intense, with lots of extra garlic and ginger. The version I have here is the one we've been making at home every Saturday since I was a child. My absolute favourite way to serve this is with Aloo Paratha or Bateta Wada and a big tablespoon of yoghurt.

INGREDIENTS

For the Daal

180 g dried whole urad daal
(black lentils)
100 g dried red beans/
azuki beans
50 g dried channa daal
(split yellow gram)
2 tsp ginger
1 ½ tsp garlic
2 green chillies
1 tbsp ghee

For the Fried Seasoning

1 tbsp ghee
2 tbsp sunflower oil
1 ½ tsp cumin
2 onions, finely chopped
1 tsp ginger
½ tsp garlic
1 green chilli, finely chopped
200 ml chopped tomatoes
Salt to taste
5 tbsp yoghurt

METHOD

• The night before making this daal, combine the black lentils, red beans, and yellow gram in a heavy pan or pressure cooker big enough to fit 2 litres of water. Thoroughly wash all the grains until the water runs clear.
• Add 1 ¼ litres of water and allow the cleaned grains to soak overnight.
• Just before cooking, add the ginger, garlic, chillies (kept whole but pricked with a fork), and ghee to the cooker.
• Place the pan over a high heat and stir the contents well to melt the ghee, mix in all the flavours, and ensure nothing is stuck to the bottom of the cooker.
• Lock the lid onto the pressure cooker or cover the pan, turn the heat down to medium, and allow to boil for 45 minutes, reducing the heat after some time if you need to.
• When the cooking time is up, turn off the heat but leave the pan covered or locked to allow all the steam to slowly diffuse, as the lentils will continue to cook as the steam dissipates.
• When all of the steam has been released, carefully uncover the pan and check that the lentils are tender – if they are not, then add a little more water and cook for longer.
• Once you are satisfied that the lentils are thoroughly cooked through, leave them to simmer over a low heat while you prepare the Tadka.
• For the Tadka, heat the oil in a frying pan placed over a medium-high temperature and add the cumin.
• When the cumin begins to fizz, add the onions and cook, stirring occasionally, until they begin to brown.
• Add the ginger, garlic, and chilli, and cook the mixture until the onions become golden, then add the tomatoes and salt.
• Cook the mixture down, stirring frequently, until the moisture evaporates from the tomatoes and you have a thick paste. Turn off the heat.
• Stir the paste into the warm daal in the pressure cooker and bring to the boil over a medium heat to allow the flavours to combine well.
• Turn off the heat and allow the daal to cool a little before stirring in the yoghurt just before serving. Eat alongside rice, paratha, or my favourites as detailed in the recipe introduction.

Kadhi
(Serves 6)

This light, yoghurt-based broth is another North Indian classic, and is served in a variety of ways across different regions. Punjabi Kadhi is usually a little thicker than others and features the addition of pakoras which absorb some of the liquid and make the broth more substantial. Gujarati Kadhi is a little thinner, and made slightly sweet by adding jaggery. Instead of pakoras, it sometimes includes chopped okra to make it into more of a meal in its own right. Although it is yoghurt-based, the warming cinnamon and cloves in the recipe make it ideal for the winter, which is when Mum most often makes this version. It's thin and slightly sweet in the Gujarati style, but with a welcome sour punch from the yoghurt. Serve with biryani or pilau rice for a simple-but-stunning flavourful supper.

INGREDIENTS

450 g slightly sour yoghurt
30 g gram flour
840 ml water
½ tbsp ghee OR sunflower oil
7 curry leaves
½ tsp cumin
3 cloves
3 cm cinnamon bark, crushed
Pinch of asafoetida
¼ tsp turmeric
1 tbsp ginger
1 green chilli, finely chopped
1 ½ tbsp jaggery OR sugar
Small handful of fresh coriander to garnish

METHOD

• Add the yoghurt to a saucepan and sift in the gram flour. Pour in 240 ml of the water, ensuring it is cold so that no lumps form, and whisk together until frothy and smooth.
• Heat the ghee in a pan placed over a medium temperature, and then add the curry leaves, cumin, cloves, cinnamon, and asafoetida. Wait for the spices to get hot and start fizzing in the pan to release their flavours before proceeding.
• Remove the pan from the heat. Very carefully, pour the yoghurt mixture into the pan, followed by the remaining water, whisking constantly (or else the mixture will split or turn lumpy – just like when making custard).
• Return the pan to the medium heat and add the turmeric, ginger, chilli, and jaggery.
• Turn the heat up to medium-high and bring the mixture to the boil, whisking continuously.
• Reduce the heat to medium and allow the Kadhi to simmer as you stir it for 5 more minutes (you can ease the whisking to a stir at this stage).
• Serve hot, sprinkled with fresh coriander, alongside your favourite rice dish.

BREADS

Unleavened breads are a key feature of Indian cuisine. They are almost always served alongside Indian meals, but often overlooked as they are not the star of the show. Served alongside curries and daals, breads make delicious compliments to the punchy spices in the gravies. The selection of Indian breads has increased vastly in recent years, with some restaurants using their diverse varieties as a unique selling point to attract customers. In this section, I'll show you all my family favourites. Once you've mastered these, it won't be long before you start experimenting with your own flavours.

Rotis/Chapattis
(Serves 6)

Perhaps the most common Indian flatbreads, these are made almost daily in my home alongside everyday curries and daals. They are wholesome, fairly quick and easy to make -and absolutely delicious served hot.

INGREDIENTS

250 g wholewheat/chapatti flour, plus extra for dusting
2 tbsp sunflower oil
125 ml warm water
½ tsp extra sunflower oil
Ghee or butter, optional

METHOD

• Add the flour to a large mixing bowl and drizzle the oil on top.
• Pour about half of the water into the flour and begin to knead, adding more water as and when required. You might not need all of it, or you may need slightly more, depending on your flour.
• Knead into soft, stretchy dough – it should still very slightly stick to your hands at this point.
• Moisten your hands with about half a teaspoon more of oil, and knead this into the dough to make it smooth and no longer sticky.
• Allow the dough to rest for about 15 minutes. In the meantime, place a heavy skillet over a medium heat to warm.
• After 15 minutes, return to your dough. Fold it over itself a couple of times to loosen it up slightly.
• Take a piece of dough roughly the size of a ping pong ball, roll it between your palms until smooth, and lightly dust it with some of the extra flour.
• Place the small ball of dough on a flat, flour-dusted surface and use a rolling pin to roll into a circle about 15-16 cm in diameter (and 2 mm in thickness). Lightly dust the dough in more flour if it sticks to the surface or the rolling pin and use a light touch. You do not want to press the dough out, but gently ease it into a circle.
• Carefully pick up your Chapatti and place it onto the hot skillet. Allow it to cook for about a minute, or until the surface facing you turns light pink and starts to form small bubbles on top.
• Using a spatula, carefully lift and flip the Chapatti.
• Cook on the second side until it becomes golden brown, and then carefully flip the Chapatti once more.
• Use a rolled up tea towel to gently press around the top edge of the Chapatti – this should cause it to puff into a ball and will make a nice soft flatbread.
• When the Chapatti is golden brown on both sides it is ready. Spread a little ghee or butter on one side if you like, and enjoy served hot alongside some daal or curry.

Tip: If you have a gas hob and are up for the challenge, on the third flip, turn the Chapatti directly onto a low flame. Quickly and carefully increase the flame to medium for a few seconds, using tongs to manoeuvre the Chapatti and make sure it is evenly cooked. Reduce the heat again and remove the Chapatti from the flame before serving for an even more authentic home-cooked Indian taste.

Paratha

(Serves 6)

These flatbreads are similar to Chapattis, but are layered and fried to make them wonderfully flaky. They are great on their own dipped into pickles, chutneys, or Masala Chai for breakfast; alternatively, serve them with thick daal for a wholesome lunch or dinner.

INGREDIENTS

500g whole wheat or chapatti flour, plus more for dusting
1 tsp salt
1 tsp black pepper
3 tbsp sunflower oil, plus more for layering and frying
400 ml warm water

METHOD

• To make the Paratha dough, add the flour, salt, and pepper to a large mixing bowl, then drizzle in the oil and roughly mix it into the flour.
• Pour half of the water into the flour and knead to begin forming the dough. Add remaining water as and when you need it until you are left with a smooth, soft-but-dry dough – you may not need all the water, or you might need a little more, depending on your flour.
• Leave the dough to rest for 15 minutes and, in the meantime, place a heavy skillet to heat up over a medium heat.
• After 15 minutes, turn the dough over itself a few times to make it easier to work with.
• Take a golf ball-sized amount and roll into a smooth ball.
• Place the ball of dough on a flat, flour-dusted surface and use a rolling pin to roll it into a circle about 10 cm in diameter. Lightly dust the dough in more flour if it sticks to the surface or the rolling pin. Handle the dough lightly - you do not want to press the dough out, just gently ease it into a circle.
• Dip a teaspoon in some of the extra oil and use the back of the spoon to moisten the surface of the rolled Paratha. Leave a 5 mm border around the edge of the Paratha dry, so that it will stick to itself when folded over.
• Fold the circle in half so that you have hidden the oiled surface, and then moisten the top of this semi-circle with oil as before, again leaving a dry border around the edge.
• Fold the semi-circle in half, hiding the oiled surface. You will be left with a small triangle of dough.
• Lightly dust the triangle with a little more flour and then roll out once more into an approximately 15 cm wide, 3 mm thick triangle, dusting with more flour if and when required.
• Carefully lift up the Paratha and place it onto the hot skillet. Allow the Paratha to cook on this side for about 30-45 seconds, until the top surface starts to bubble and the bottom side looks like it's just beginning to turn golden.
• Carefully flip the Paratha and allow to cook for 30 seconds more. Spread a little oil over the surface before flipping again.
• Fry for 30 seconds on this side before spreading the surface with a little more oil and flipping the Paratha for the last time.
• Cook until golden on both sides and then transfer onto a cooling rack to stop it from going soggy while you roll and fry the remaining Parathas.
• Roll and fry the remaining dough following the above procedure – if you find you have more dough than you need, you can wrap it in cling film and keep it in the fridge for up to a day.
• Serve hot or cold with curries or pickles... or even a cup of tea.

Thepla
(Serves 6)

Thepla are like a lightly-spiced version of Parathas. They are traditionally served with Masala Chai at breakfast, or alternatively, paired with a simple, delicately-flavoured dry curry for lunch, or packed for picnics and long journeys.

INGREDIENTS

250 g fresh fenugreek leaves
2 green chillies, finely chopped
1 tbsp garlic
1 tbsp ginger
4 tbsp sunflower oil, plus more for frying
2 tsp carom seeds
Salt to taste
Large pinch of asafoetida
½ tsp turmeric powder
100 g gram flour
200 g millet flour
250 g chapatti/plain flour, plus more for dusting
80 g cooked rice (optional)
125 ml warm water
150 ml double cream

METHOD

• Roughly chop the fenugreek leaves, wash them, and allow the excess water to drain away. Transfer to a mixing bowl.
• Add the chillies, garlic, ginger, 4 tbsp oil, carom seeds, salt, asafoetida, and turmeric, and then mix everything together.
• Add the flours (and rice, if using) and mix once more before gradually adding enough water to form smooth-but-stiff dough.
• Leave the dough to rest for 15 minutes. In the meantime, place a heavy skillet over a medium heat to warm up. Take a golf ball-sized amount of the dough and roll into a smooth ball.
• Dust in chapatti or plain flour and gently roll out into a circle approximately 10 cm in diameter and 3 mm thick, lightly dusting in more flour if the dough begins to stick as you are rolling it.
• Place the rolled-out Thepla onto the hot skillet and increase the heat to medium-high. When the dough begins to bubble slightly on the surface, use a spatula to help you lift and flip it over.
• Allow the Thepla to cook for about 20 seconds on the second side before lightly drizzling the surface facing you with a little oil.
• Flip the Thepla again so that the oiled side can fry. Wait 20 more seconds before drizzling the top with oil again, and then flip for the last time, so that the Thepla is evenly fried on both sides.
• Drain on kitchen paper and repeat with the remaining dough.
• Serve alongside tea or pickles, or use as a wrap for dry curries.

Puri

(Makes 6)

These fluffy, spiced balloons of fried pastry are light and moreish. Most commonly served with Masala Chai or basic potato curry, they are quick and easy to make - and look delightful when stacked up in a big serving bowl.

INGREDIENTS

250 g whole wheat/chapatti flour, plus extra for dusting
50 g gram flour
Salt to taste
1 tsp red chilli powder
½ tsp turmeric
½ tsp carom seeds
Small pinch of asafoetida
3 ½ tbsp sunflower oil, plus more for deep-frying
100 ml warm water

METHOD

• Add both of the flours to a large mixing bowl and mix in the salt, chilli powder, turmeric, carom seeds and asafoetida.
• Drizzle in the oil and lightly rub into the flour mixture.
• Pour in half of the water and begin to knead the flour to form the dough. Add more water as required – you might not need it all – to form fairly dry, smooth dough.
• Leave to rest for 20 minutes. In the meantime heat up oil for deep frying in a wok or karahi placed over a medium heat.
• Portion the dough into walnut sized segments and then, dusting with flour as required, roll into circles approximately 10 cm diameter by 2 mm thick.
• Fry the Puris in hot oil. Place the rolled circles of dough into the oil one at a time, and gently press with a skimmer or slotted spoon until they puff (this should only take a maximum of 20 seconds). Once puffed, turn the Puri in the oil and fry until golden on both sides.
• Strain and remove from the oil, and place onto kitchen paper to drain completely.
• Serve hot.

Naan

(Serves 6)

Naan are traditional North Indian flatbreads. Unlike most other Indian bread recipes, these are normally leavened with yoghurt or yeast to make soft, stretchy, puffy dough. However, rather than baked as loaves, the dough is segmented and stretched out in a similar way to pizza dough. The resulting flat naan are light, crispy, and just a little spongy in places.

INGREDIENTS

250 g chapatti or plain flour
1 tbsp sugar
½ tsp salt
1 tbsp sunflower oil
50 ml yoghurt
100 ml warm water

METHOD

- Sift the flour into a large mixing bowl and stir in the sugar and salt.
- Add the oil and yoghurt and mix well.
- Gradually add the water – first add half, and then only add as much more as you require while you knead the dough on a lightly floured surface for 10 minutes until it is soft and stretchy without being sticky.
- Place the dough in a lightly oiled bowl, cover with a damp tea towel, and leave to rest in a warm place for 1 hour.
- After the hour is up, place a heavy non-stick frying pan to heat over a medium-high setting. Have to hand a lid that fits over the top.
- Gently fold the dough over itself a few times and divide into 6.
- On a floured surface, gently roll a portion of dough into a circle about 11 cm in diameter and 1 cm thick, and then use your hands to shape it into the signature 'tear-drop' naan shape. This should also help thin down the naan to a thickness of around 5 mm.
- Spread the surface of the Naan with a little water and carefully place it, damp-side-down, onto the hot skillet, and cover.
- Allow to cook for about 30 seconds, until the top surface starts to bubble, and then use a spatula to lift and flip the Naan over.
- Allow to cook on the second side until golden brown, remove from the pan, and serve hot with butter spread generously on top.

Tip: Spice up the Naan by using it as a pizza base – simply spread one side with thick chilli and garlic chutney, add your favourite toppings, and grill until golden.

Stuffed Paratha

(Serves 6)

These stuffed flatbreads are incredibly popular with their crispy, flaky pastry and succulent, moist filling. You can make the filling from a variety of ingredients including mixed vegetables and beans, but in my own experience, it's the potato-stuffed (aloo) parathas that prove most popular. They're certainly an enduring Rawal family favourite.

INGREDIENTS

For the Stuffing

1 ½ kg potatoes, boiled
and peeled
Salt to taste
1 tbsp sugar
Juice of half a lemon
2 ½ tsp ginger
2 green chillies, finely chopped
½ tsp turmeric
½ tsp red chilli powder
Small handful of fresh
coriander leaves,
finely chopped

For the Parathas

500 g whole wheat or chapatti
flour, plus more for dusting
1 tsp salt
2 tbsp sunflower oil
500 ml warm water
Oil for shallow-frying

METHOD

• For the stuffing, mash the potatoes and add all of the remaining ingredients for the filling. Mix well to create a smooth, well-seasoned mixture. Leave aside.
• To make the paratha dough, add the flour and salt to a large mixing bowl. Drizzle in the oil and roughly mix it into the flour.
• Pour half of the water into the flour and knead to begin forming the dough. Add the remaining water as and when you need it until you are left with smooth, soft, moist dough – you may not need all the water, or you might need a little more, depending on your flour. If the dough is too dry, it will be difficult to stuff with the filling, and keeping it slightly moist will allow it to remain more elastic.
• Leave the dough to rest for 15 minutes. In the meantime, place a heavy skillet to warm up over a medium heat.
• After 15 minutes, turn the dough over itself a few times to make it easier to work with, then take a golf ball-sized amount and roll into a smooth ball.
• Place the ball of dough on a flat, flour-dusted surface and use a rolling pin to roll it into a circle about 10 cm in diameter. Lightly dust the dough in more flour if it sticks to the surface or the rolling pin. Use a light touch - you do not want to press the dough out, merely gently ease it into a circle.
• Take about 2 tablespoons of the potato mixture and roll it into a smooth ball, then slightly flatten it before placing in the middle of the circle of dough.
• Bring the sides of the dough up to the top centre of the squashed ball of potato filling so that the entire filling is encased and you have a small knot of dough at the top.
• Carefully, ensuring that the wrap of dough around the filling does not tear, break the top knot from the ball and add it back to the remaining dough (if you leave this piece of dough on the Paratha it will be too thick to cook through, and all your efforts will be ruined).
• Gently press down the gathers at the top of the ball, and flatten to form a disc 1-2 cm thick.
• Dust the disc with a little more flour, turn it over and then gradually roll out the Paratha to approximately 16-18 cm in diameter, and 6 mm in thickness (dust with more flour as you roll if necessary).
• Carefully lift up the Paratha and place it onto the hot skillet. Ideally, you want the side that was facing you whilst rolling to remain topper most whilst cooking, so that the other, slightly thicker side where you formed the seal gets properly cooked through.
• Allow the Paratha to cook on this side for about 30-45 seconds, until the top surface starts to bubble and the bottom side looks like it's just beginning to turn golden.
• Carefully flip the Paratha, allow to cook for a further 30 seconds, and then spread a little oil over the surface before flipping again.
• Fry for 30 seconds on this side, before spreading the top surface with a little more oil and flipping for the last time.
• Cook until golden on both sides, and then transfer onto some kitchen roll to drain off any excess oil.
• Serve hot with yoghurt, chutneys, or, my favourite – daal makhani.

DESSERTS

A proper dinner party wouldn't be complete without a sweet little ending, and of course I'm well known for my love of sweet food. The desserts in this chapter are all perfect sweet finales to the flavourful recipes presented in this book – refreshing without overpowering, and, naturally, gorgeous to look at.

Saffron Semifreddo

(Serves 8)

This ice cream-like dish is one of my favourite summer desserts to make. It has all the flavours of traditional Indian Malai Kulfi, but is light, effortless, and looks beautiful. For something that only takes a few moments to prepare, and requires only a handful of ingredients, it is truly sensational – your family and friends will love it.

INGREDIENTS

1 tbsp chopped pistachio nuts (optional)
1 tbsp chopped almonds (optional)
½ tsp saffron threads
1 x 394 g tin sweetened condensed milk
Juice of 1 lemon
400 ml double cream
¼ tsp ground green cardamom

METHOD

• Line a 10 x 20 cm loaf tin with cling film, and sprinkle the nuts into the lined base of the tin. Keep aside.
• Gently dry-roast the saffron threads in a dry frying pan until they become fragrant and then leave aside to cool – this step helps them impart more flavour when added to the recipe.
• Pour the contents of the tin of condensed milk into a large mixing bowl, add the lemon juice, and whisk briskly until thickened.
• Pour the cream into the thickened condensed milk, and whisk until it forms soft peaks.
• Crumble the saffron over the cream, sprinkle in the cardamom, and gently fold into the mixture.
• Pour the mixture into the prepared loaf tin and freeze overnight.
• Just before serving, remove the loaf tin from the freezer and use the cling film to help you gently turn the semifreddo out onto a serving dish.
• Remove the cling film, and garnish with fresh fruit if desired (mango works wonderfully).

> Tip: As this recipe is a true semifreddo, it will literally only half-freeze – there's no need to leave it out to defrost slightly, just cut through it with a sharp knife and serve immediately.

Chocolate Shrikhand
(Serves 8)

This thick and creamy sweetened yoghurt dessert is great after a spicy meal. The slight tang from the yoghurt really brings out the chocolate flavour, which in turn works beautifully with the pistachio nuts. A little of this indulgent pudding goes a long way, so it is ideal for guests who prefer just a small dessert serving.

INGREDIENTS

500 g thick set yoghurt
150 g good quality milk or dark chocolate
350 g icing sugar
4 tblsp dry roasted pistachio nuts, finely chopped
1 tsp ground cardamom

METHOD

• The night before you require this dessert, turn the yoghurt out onto a muslin or cheesecloth, tie it up, and let it hang from a tap overnight so that any excess liquid can drain away.
• The next morning, gently melt the chocolate either in a heatproof bowl placed above a pan of simmering water (don't let the water touch the bottom of the bowl), or in the microwave, stirring it every few seconds until melted. Leave aside to cool.
• Set out serving bowls or glasses ready to spoon the pudding into once it is mixed.
• Turn the strained yoghurt out into a large mixing bowl and beat until smooth.
• Sift the icing sugar over the yoghurt and mix together.
• Gently fold the chocolate into the yoghurt mixture until it is evenly mixed through and the shrikhand is smooth-textured.
• Fold the pistachio nuts and cardamom through the mixture, and then spoon or pipe into the prepared serving bowls or glasses.
• Keep refrigerated until required and serve chilled.

Kheer Pakora

(Serves 6)

The Indian version of rice pudding – kheer - is a firm favourite at home, and so are the rice pakoras – fulavra - mentioned earlier in this book. It just made sense to combine the two and see what would happen – and we were not disappointed! These wispy nuggets are crispy on the outside and deliciously creamy and sweet in the middle, almost like tiny doughnuts. I highly recommend giving this a go, especially as a sweet for a special occasion.

INGREDIENTS

For the Kheer Pakoras

500 ml whole milk
50g pudding rice
¼ tsp ghee
40g caster sugar, plus extra for dusting
¼ tsp crushed saffron threads
1 tbsp chopped pistachio nuts
100 ml single cream

For the Dipping Sauce:

¼ tsp crushed saffron threads
¾ tsp ground cardamom
100g apricot jam

For the Pakora Batter:

4 tbsp plain flour
Oil for deep-frying

METHOD

• Set the milk to warm in a heavy-based saucepan over a medium heat.
• While the milk warms, rinse the rice in cold water, roughly dry the grains and rub in the ghee, making sure all of the grains are lightly coated.
• When the milk is hot, add the rice to it and allow to cook until completely tender, about 20 – 30 minutes over a medium heat.
• Stir in the sugar, saffron, and all of the cream, and bring to the boil over a medium-low heat, stirring continuously until the liquid evaporates and the kheer is well-thickened.
• Stir in ½ tsp of the cardamom.
• Switch off the heat and spread the kheer onto a greased baking sheet. Cover with cling film, ensuring the film is pressed onto the kheer to stop it from forming a skin as it cools.
• Chill the kheer until it is firm enough to roll into balls.
• Roll tablespoon amounts of the kheer into smooth balls, place back onto the baking tray, and freeze for at least 1 hour or until just before ready to serve.
• In the meantime, make the dipping sauce by warming the apricot jam with 50 ml water and stirring in the saffron and cardamom. When well-combined, remove the sauce from the heat and pour into a serving bowl.
• When you are ready to fry the kheer balls, place some oil for deep-frying into a karahi or wok and heat over a medium-high setting.
• Prepare the batter for the pakora by mixing the flour with just enough water to make a smooth, runny batter for coating the balls in.
• Dip the kheer balls, 3 or 4 at a time, into the batter, and fry until golden. Drain on kitchen paper and toss in extra caster sugar for a textured effect.
• Serve hot alongside the dipping sauce.

Sweet Vermicelli
(Serves 6)

This dessert is popular in the North of India, and is usually served during special occasions and festivals due to the inclusion of dried fruits and nuts which are considered extremely prestigious and regal. The vermicelli, known as 'Seviyan', can also be made as a kheer, cooked in sweetened milk, but I love this version which is super-delicious and, as a bonus, super-speedy!

INGREDIENTS

1 tbsp ghee
200 g vermicelli noodles, broken into 4 cm pieces
400 ml water
100 g caster sugar
½ tsp saffron strands
10 g raisins
20 g almonds
10 g pistachios
¼ tsp ground cardamom

METHOD

• Heat the ghee in a large wok or karahi placed over a medium-high temperature, then add the vermicelli and roast in the ghee until golden brown.
• Carefully pour the water into the pan, and stir in the saffron and raisins.
• Cook until the water evaporates, then stir in the sugar which will melt down into a liquid. Cook the mixture down until almost dry before adding the almonds and pistachios.
• Cook until the seviyan is dry and crispy, turn off the heat, and stir in the cardamom.
• Serve warm.

Apple Jalebi

(Serves 6)

Jalebi are the vibrant, orange-coloured gram flour swirls found in most Indian sweet shops. They are crunchy and super-sweet, with a hint of sourness which comes from the fermented yoghurt batter. This version, made with apples, is a little less sweet for those who find traditional jalebi too overpowering. These are far easier to make, and are fairly instant compared to the traditional method, which requires hours of fermenting.

INGREDIENTS

For the Syrup

200 g caster sugar
250 ml water
½ tsp saffron threads

For the Apple Jalebi

300 g plain flour
½ tbsp fruit salts such as Eno
OR 1 tbsp bicarbonate of soda
2 Granny Smith apples, peeled, cored and sliced into 5 mm thick circles
Sunflower oil for deep-frying
Sliced pistachio nuts to garnish

METHOD

• To begin with, prepare the sugar syrup. Place the sugar in a heavy pan and pour in the water, add the saffron, and leave to heat over a medium temperature. Once the sugar has dissolved, stir occasionally until the syrup just begins to become sticky. Turn off the heat.
• While the sugar syrup is cooking, heat the oil in a wok or karahi over a medium-high setting.
• Prepare the batter for the jalebi by whisking the plain flour with water until it becomes smooth and reaches the same consistency as pancake batter.
• When the oil is ready, whisk the fruit salts or bicarbonate of soda into the batter, and dip the apple slices into it one at a time, before deep-frying in the hot oil.
• Fry the battered apple slices for about a minute, until golden and crisp on both sides.
•Drain on kitchen paper and then, whilst still warm, let the fritters soak in the warm sugar syrup for 1 minute before placing on a serving plate and garnishing with pistachios.
• Serve warm, ideally with ice cream.

DRINKS

Drinks served with - or after - Indian meals serve very specific purposes. They are not only hydrating and cooling in the scorching Indian heat; they also help to ease the digestion of spicy curries. Mostly milky, refreshing, or sweet – they are always fragrant and delicious!

Lassi
(Serves 5)

This cooling yoghurt-based beverage is one of the most popular served all across India, especially in the North, and it comes in a variety of flavours. The most traditional savoury varieties are lightly-salted, and are vital to help replace salts lost from the body during hot weather. This flavoursome version adds a punch of roasted cumin that helps aid digestion and adds a delicious smoky flavour to the lassi.

INGREDIENTS

500 ml yoghurt
3 tsp roasted cumin, ground
750 ml water
Salt to taste

METHOD

• Add the yoghurt to a mixing bowl and sprinkle in the roasted cumin powder. Beat until smooth.
• Whisk in the water, adding salt to taste, until the mixture is well blended and frothy.
• Cover and chill until required. Serve over ice.

Tip: To make the most popular sweet variety, take 3 ripe large mangoes or a tin of mango pulp, 400 ml yoghurt, 1 tsp freshly ground cardamom, and 500 ml water. If using fresh fruits, peel the mangoes and scrape the flesh from the stone. Beat the mango with the yoghurt and cardamom until smooth. Whisk in the water until the mixture becomes the consistency of a thin milkshake – or keep it thick, if you prefer it that way. Whisk in a little sugar to sweeten the taste if desired. Cover, chill, and serve over ice.

Indian Lemonade
(Serves 5)

This refreshing, cooling cocktail – Nimbu Pani – is the Indian version of lemonade. It can be made with still or sparkling water and is seriously hydrating. If made with tonic water it can almost serve as a non-alcoholic substitute for gin and tonic! Indian lemons are small and round – they look similar to limes, and the flavour is a cross between the two. They pack a sour punch with a slightly sweet edge. If you can't get hold of Indian lemons, use a combination of lemons and limes.

INGREDIENTS

5 Indian lemons (or a mixture of lemons and limes)
A small handful of fresh mint leaves
50 g caster sugar
1 tsp roasted cumin, ground
Black salt OR regular salt to taste
750 ml water

METHOD

• Juice the lemons into a mixing jug, making sure to remove any seeds.
• Add the mint leaves, sugar, roasted cumin, and salt, and then muddle everything together using the end of a rolling pin or wooden spoon to extract and combine flavours.
• Whisk in the water and check the seasoning – adding a little more sugar or lemon if desired.
• Serve well-chilled, over ice.

Fennel Water

(Serves 5)

According to Ayurvedic medicine a spectrum of health benefits are attributed to fennel, known as 'saunf' or 'valyari' in India. I can't vouch for the health properties, but I can, with great conviction, say that this super-simple drink is palate-cleansing, breath-freshening, and wonderful for digestion. Traditionally, the fennel is boiled with the water, but I like to steep it overnight for a more subtle flavour. The ginger is optional but really adds to the beautiful flavour of this drink.

INGREDIENTS

100 g fennel seeds
2 tsp ginger
750 ml water
Sugar to taste

METHOD

• Ensure your fennel seeds are clean by giving them a wash, then place them into the bottom of a large, lidded jar, or a mixing bowl.
• Add the ginger and pour in the water.
• If using a jar with a lid, then place the lid on and give the jar a good shake for a minute or two, allowing the spices to infuse in the water and release their flavours. Alternatively, whisk the mixture thoroughly in the mixing bowl, encouraging all of the flavours to mingle.
• Refrigerate overnight and, when you are ready to serve, mix in a little sugar to taste and pour into chilled glasses. Serve cold.

Falooda

(Serves 4)

This dessert drink originates from Pakistan, but is now a common offering alongside the street food stalls in Mumbai. The milk and basil seeds are cooling, whilst the ice cream and vermicelli thicken the dessert to a milkshake-like consistency. Rose and cardamom flavours make the liquid soothing and calming – providing perfect respite from the Mumbai madness!

INGREDIENTS

1 L milk – almond milk works just as well as dairy for this recipe
Sugar to taste
2 tbsp basil seeds
20 g vermicelli, snapped into 2.5 cm pieces
4 tbsp rose syrup
½ tsp ground cardamom
Vanilla ice cream and chopped pistachios to serve

METHOD

• Pour the milk into a heavy pan and bring to the boil over a medium heat.
• Stir in the sugar, basil seeds, and vermicelli, and simmer over a medium-high heat for 15 minutes.
• Turn off the heat and stir in the rose syrup.
• Allow the milk to cool slightly before stirring in the cardamom.
• Leave to chill for a few hours in the refrigerator.
• Serve cold, in tall glasses filled with ice, topped with a scoop of ice cream and a scattering of chopped pistachios.

Masala Chai

(Serves 2)

Possibly the most well-known beverage from India, Masala Chai or 'spiced tea' is served throughout India, all day, every day. The concept of drinking tea was actually introduced to Indians by the British, but the idea has stuck and, in true Indian style, it has been developed with the addition of a variety of spice blends. The actual spice blends themselves vary from household to household, with each person flavouring their tea to their own taste, or using the spices they feel are most beneficial to their wellbeing. Most commonly, they include ginger, cardamom, cloves, cinnamon, mace, and fennel. This version, using freshly-ground whole spices, is our favourite at home. If you love tea, then please experiment using your favourite spices and flavours to find your own perfect cup.

INGREDIENTS

1 tsp ground cinnamon
½ tsp ground ginger
¼ tsp ground cloves
¼ tsp ground cardamom
350 ml water
4 tsp loose black tea
175 ml milk
Sugar to taste

METHOD

• Combine all of the ground spices together and grind them further – allowing the flavours to blend with one another.
• Prepare 4 cup-and-saucer sets, and place a tea strainer over one set.
• Heat the water in a saucepan over a medium heat then add the tea leaves.
• Allow the tea to come to a boil before reducing the heat slightly and adding the milk and spices (and sugar if desired). Stir and wait for the tea to come to the boil once more.
• Reduce the heat further and simmer for 1 minute.
• Turn off the heat and then strain the tea directly into the first cup, transferring the strainer to the next cup and pouring the tea into each in turn.
• Serve very hot, at breakfast, tea-time, after a meal...or whenever you fancy a soothing pick-me-up.

Printed in Great Britain
by Amazon.co.uk, Ltd.,
Marston Gate.